open

open

open

editorial

JORINDE SEIJDEL

2030: WAR ZONE AMSTERDAM

Imagining the Unimaginable

Open is conducting structural
research into the current conditions
of public space and changing notions
of publicness. This implies an experimental and interdisciplinary expo-
sition of the reality, possibilities
and limitations of contemporary urban
space, notably from sociological,
philosophical, political and artistic perspectives. Within the scope
of this 'project in progress', themes
such as safety, memory, visibility, cultural freedom, tolerance,
hybrid space, the rise of informal
media, art as a public issue, social
engineering and precarity have come
up. When *Open* was approached by
the independent Amsterdam curator
Brigitte van der Sande about working
together on an issue of this journal
whose contents would tie in with an
art event she is organizing, *2030:
War Zone Amsterdam*, this presented a
chance to further these explorations
and editorial goals.

    2030: War Zone Amsterdam as per-
ceived by Van der Sande will be an
exercise in imagining the unimaginable: civil war in Amsterdam in the
year 2030. This subject, no matter
how absurd it may seem, immediately
prickled the imagination of the edi-

tors. Extrapolating an extreme situation to a near future, and turning
the city of Amsterdam into a concrete case and a projection screen,
makes it possible to continue, spec-
ify and sharpen *Open*'s reflection on
a number of fundamental and urgent
topics. Moreover, the fictitious
element presents the contemporary
social reality of Amsterdam, which
shows little creative development in
the debates on some social issues,
in a radically different light.

    What must be emphasized, however,
is that no enemies are named in *2030:
War Zone Amsterdam*. Rather, it is an
intensified impression of an actual
urban space in which certain social,
historical, co-political, cultural
and urban conditions are magni-
fied. Neither do all of the contributions in *Open* 18 literally refer to
Amsterdam. Some essays take a more
global approach in analysing significant developments and scenarios of
the future with respect to the contemporary city and/or forms of warfare. Using Amsterdam as a test case,
this issue of *Open* ultimately is
about questions and problems gener-
ally facing Western cities today:
fear and safety, privacy and biopolitics, control and militarization,
globalization and virtualization,
commercialization and neoliberalism.

In the introduction to *Open* 18,
guest editor Brigitte van der Sande

explains her motives and the history that is behind *2030: War Zone Amsterdam*, and partly also behind this issue, under the motto 'There is no audience, there are only participants'. The Rotterdam sociologist Willem Schinkel discusses the implications of an urban policy for Amsterdam that employs war rhetoric and marketing strategies. In a fictional contribution, the novelist and philosopher Dirk van Weelden imagines what it is like to live and move about in an Amsterdam at war. The British Frank Furedi, author of *Politics of Fear* (2005), analyzes the politicization and dramatization of fear. He calls upon Amsterdam to conduct a public discussion in which the participants are not the objects but the subjects of change. John Armitage interviewed the philosopher and urbanist Paul Virilio on the contemporary conditions of the city in relation to the concept of war zone for *Open*. Virilio speaks of 'cities beyond the city' that are anchored in the electromagnetic waves of increasingly faster information and communications technologies. Stephen Graham, whose work on the one hand investigates the relationships between urban locales, mobility, infrastructure and technology, and war, surveillance and geopolitics on the other, is interviewed by Bryan Finoki on his viewpoints. In the column, writer Tom McCarthy rakes up an Amsterdam experience in which Mexico City, Dante's *Inferno* and *The Fall* by Camus converge. Starting from the concept

of 'urbanibalism', Wietske Maas and Matteo Pasquinelli test the edibility of the city in times of war. Among other things, they search for Amsterdam's hidden 'third landscape of food'. In architect and theoretician Eyal Weizman's adapted article, he uses an interview with two brigadier generals of the Israeli Armed Forces to illustrate the importance of theories derived from figures such as Tschumi, Deleuze and Guattari for recent ways of conducting war. Weizman wonders what the implications of this deadly theory are for the city and its inhabitants.

This issue also includes artists' contributions by Gert Jan Kocken and the Israeli duo Adi Kaplan & Shahar Carmel. Kocken placed a large number of historical maps of Amsterdam one over the other, with their combined information trying to capture something of the city's recent war years, which are still interwoven in its present-day structure. His contribution is introduced by the art critic and historian Bianca Stigter, author of, among others, *De bezette stad. Plattegrond van Amsterdam 1940-1945*. Kaplan & Carmel visited Amsterdam and drew a cartoon speculating on a possible future based on their experiences. Imagine a city – your own city, for instance – in which everything is on edge . . .

Editorial

Brigitte
van der Sande

2030: War Zone
Amsterdam

*Introduction
to the
Manifestation*

This issue of
Open functions
as an indepen-
dent reader for
*2030: War Zone
Amsterdam*,[1] an
event that kicks
off in November
2009. Here,
Brigitte van der
Sande, curator

of the event
and guest editor
of this issue,
explains her
motives.

1. The preliminary
research for the event was
possible thanks to a grant
for intermediaries from the
Netherlands Foundation
for the Visual Arts, Design
and Architecture (Fonds
BKVB).

'There is no audience, there are only participants.'

After Joseph Kosuth

'I can't tell you what art does and how it does it, but I know that art has often judged the judges, pleaded revenge to the innocent and shown to the future what the past has suffered, so that it has never been forgotten.

'I know too that the powerful fear art, whatever its form, when it does this, and that amongst the people such art sometimes runs like a rumour and a legend because it makes sense of what life's brutalities cannot, a sense that unites us, for it is inseparable from a justice at last. Art, when it functions like this, becomes a meeting-place of the invisible, the irreducible, the enduring, guts and honour.'

John Berger

It was May of 2002 when I received a phone call while on vacation in France: Pim Fortuyn, the populist politician and Holland's most famous 'camp' gay, had just been killed, nine days before he was expected to win the parliamentary elections. In a leading article in *Le Monde* a few days later, a journalist wrote of a furious crowd marching to parliament in The Hague, suggesting that the Netherlands was on the brink of civil war. What a joke, I thought at the time. Granted, the first political murder since 1672 had turned the country upside down, but civil war in our chilly little country driven by consensus and compromise? Impossible! Just a month before the murder, however, the recently deceased cultural critic Michaël Zeeman had expressed his premonition of an approaching catastrophe: 'I do not believe in the spectre of an Islamist threat any more than I do in that of the Fortuynists as a xenophobic rabble. But it would seem to me that the idea of Dutch society being historically disinclined to instability is in need of revision. For by the look of it, there now is a nasty fissure running through society, a fissure that is only getting bigger.'[2]

2030: War Zone Amsterdam[3] is an exercise in imagining the unimaginable: civil war in your own city in the year 2030. A cease-fire has just been announced, and a group of international artists, theatre makers, filmmakers, journalists and intellectuals go out into the city to investigate what the war has done to Amsterdam and its inhabitants. *2030: War Zone Amsterdam*

2. Michaël Zeeman, *de Volkskrant*, 15 April 2002. On 22 August 2009 in *NRC Handelsblad*, author Ian Buruma also pointed out that Dutch society is divided into two camps: fearful Dutch and badgered Muslims. If this development continues, there will be blood, Buruma concluded in his article.

3. The initiative for imagining a civil war in Amsterdam in the year 2030 comes from Partizan Publik, 'a think and action tank devoted to a braver society'. They approached me in early 2007 with the idea of collaborating on their project, *Amsterdam at War*. Partizan Publik wanted to set up a virtual exhibition showing the effects of a war in the city in 2030 and I was to make a cultural contribution. We very soon decided to separate the two investigations. The starting point for both Partizan Publik and myself remains the same: civil war in Amsterdam in the year 2030. The title *Amsterdam at War* will be used by Partizan Publik. I chose the title *2030: War Zone Amsterdam* for an event that will mainly take place outside the walls of institutional art spaces.

names no enemies, provides no answers, but fires questions at a possible future. The participants occupy public space, infiltrate exhibitions, festivals and publications, or seek cover in underground spaces. *2030: War Zone Amsterdam* makes the concept of war, so abstract for the Dutch, specific and palpable by projecting the artists as well as the public onto a war situation in Amsterdam.

The enemy is unknown – for history has shown time and again that a former enemy can become a best friend. The war is deliberately situated in the city and not throughout the entire country. The character of war has changed; it no longer takes place between nation-states but between ethnic, religious or economically motivated factions that are not bound by the confines of arbitrary national borders. But what is war like in 2030? Since 9/11, a few airplanes are all it takes to plunge countries into war. Will democratic governments adapt their military strategies and, as the American journalist Robert Kaplan claims, undertake preventive actions with small groups of warriors? What tactics will people be using in urban warfare by that time? Today's and future generations are growing up with Second Life, playing virtual games and doing all sorts of virtual training. What kind of soldiers is this creating? Do they experience the reality of war in the same way that soldiers who grew up in a mechanical age did? If everybody is continuously monitored, how can the population evade virtual and physical surveillance? Through what channels do people communicate? How and where does one survive all of the violence, what is everyday life like? Is there a public domain, and what is that like? Is art still being made, and if so, how do artists reach their public? The artists participating in *2030: War Zone Amsterdam* will not answer these questions literally, but take them as a departure point for discussion of the possibilities and impossibilities of war and of the role of art.

Permanent State of Exception

Amsterdam had always been known for being an open, tolerant city where people from different cultures and backgrounds live with each other without many problems. As an Amsterdammer, I was proud of our centuries-old reputation as a haven for the religious or politically persecuted from all over the world. However, since the attacks on the Twin Towers in New York in 2001, and the murders of Pim Fortuyn in 2002 and of filmmaker Theo van Gogh in 2004, the mood in the city has changed and gradually grown harder; communities are withdrawing into their own ghettos, whether the Bijlmer, Oud-Zuid or the Bos en Lommer district. Many native Amsterdammers have become afraid of the city's Islamic residents, who in today's political reality are potential terrorists.[4] We have even

4. For a clear analysis of the developments in the Netherlands after the

become so afraid that we stand by without protest while technical infrastructure is being developed that stores all of our Internet and telephone communications, our physical movements by public transport and in the automobile, our medical records, information about our children's physical, mental and social development and so forth, and keeps it on record for years for perusal by the authorities. People in public and semi-public spaces in the city are increasingly being monitored by video cameras for suspicious movements or – even more suspicious! – for standing still.[5] And all of this is protected by a juridical infrastructure that in many respects is more far-reaching than the American Patriot Act of October 2001.[6] We are living in what Michael Hardt and Antonio Negri call a permanent state of exception, in which the right of intervention prevails – that is, the right of the police to create order and also maintain it. Laws and rights are not there to protect citizens, for everyone is suspect. No one escapes the gaze of the police, who avail themselves of every possible means to increase the effectiveness of control.[7] This takes place with the enthusiastic collaboration of the citizens, considering the success of the snitchers' telephone line *Meld Misdaad Anoniem (M.)* (Report Crime Anonymously) that was set up in 2004.[8]

So, in order to simulate discussion and get people thinking about their astonishingly laconic acceptance of the curtailment of their civil rights in the name of safety in the War on Terror, to get them thinking about the use of fear as a political element and about the direction in which we citizens want to develop our own society, this event is predicated upon a war in a conceivable future. Not because I might be war hungry or want to stir up feelings of fear. On the contrary. But indeed to stick a pin in the balloon of ease with which people in this country assume that the Netherlands will never, ever know war again because we are too reasonable and civilized for that, to debunk the assumption that war is a thing of the distant past or happens in a distant country. And to open people's eyes to a war that, according to some, has been rampant in Western society for a long time, not immediately visible and recognizable, but proliferating beneath the surface

murders of Fortuyn and Van Gogh, see Ian Buruma, *Murder in Amsterdam: The Death of Theo van Gogh and the Limits of Tolerance* (London: Atlantic Books, 2006).

5. Rick van Amersfoort, of Buro Jansen & Janssen, pointed out to me that standing still is the deviation and movement is the norm. Drifters, junkies, beggars, street musicians, and so forth automatically attract the attention of the police because of their immobility.

6. Gerhart Baum, Germany's Secretary of State and later Minister of Foreign Affairs from 1972 to 1982 describes a comparable irreversible fundamental change of the legal system in Germany in the *Tegenlicht* documentary by Alexander Oey, *Onderhandelingen met Al Queda* (Negotiations with Al Qaeda) in 2007. Politicians whipped up the fear of terrorist attacks by the Rote Armee Fraktion in order to limit civil rights, all in the name of security. The US Patriot Act stands for 'Uniting and Strengthening America by Providing Appropriate Tools Required to Intercept and Obstruct Terrorism Act'.

7. Michael Hardt and Antonio Negri, *Empire* (Cambridge, MA/London: Harvard University Press, 2000), 17 et seq. Also see the article by Willem Schinkel elsewhere in this issue.

8. In the first year, 100,000 calls led to the solving of 485 crimes. The daily paper *Trouw*, 11 February 2005. Also see http://www.meldmisdaadanoniem.nl//Articles.aspx?id=203.

like an insidious growth, popping up at unexpected places and unexpected moments.[9]

Representing and Portraying War

Anyone looking into how war is represented in the media and the arts[10] knows that the strict distinction between the supposedly objective character of the reportage in the media and the subjective portrayal of war in the arts has in the meantime been erased. As is often said, the media have from their very beginning not only recorded but also manipulated images and information in order to increase the impact, to magnify the *truth* of the news.[11] After a century of isolation in the ivory tower of *l'art pour l'art*, many artists in their turn are using the media in order to relate to the outside world. Mediatization of reality is then the departure point, not war itself. Paul Virilio traces the beginning of this development to long before the era of television, namely, to Géricault's *The Raft of the Medusa*, in 1818. With this painting,

9. This has not only been pointed out by thinkers such as Peter Sloterdijk and Negri and Hardt, but also by several of the participating artists independently of each other during discussions over the past year.

10. This topic was also the basis of my exhibition 'Soft Target. War as a Daily, First-Hand Reality', in 2005 at Basis Actuele Kunst (BAK) in Utrecht within the framework of *Concerning War*. Also see: Jordan Crandall, ed., *Under Fire 1: The Organization and Representation of Violence* (Rotterdam: Witte de With, 2004); two contributions to chapter 7, 'Assemblages of Image', 'Action and Event', 79 and 81-82.

11. See my essay 'Truth and Lies in War and Art', in the catalogue *Signals in the Dark: Art in the Shadow of War* (Blackwood Gallery and Justina M. Barnicke Gallery, University of Toronto at Mississauga, Canada, 2008), 97-103.

art entered the world of news technology. Not only was the inspiration for the painting a political commotion, the painting itself became a political commotion. The tele-presence replaces the real presence of the work of art, according to Virilio. Just like the daily paper that is used for wrapping fish the following day, the art work loses its value, its quality as a unique and rare object.[12]

What significance the arts can still have in the portrayal of war, in the portrayal of reality, is a question that has occupied me as a curator for years. How do we restore the power of the image in an era in which the creation of images long since has ceased to be reserved for professionals? How do you reach a public that either passively turns away from, or actively immerses itself in, the oversupply of spectacle, emotion and entertainment? Can we break through the appearance of things and replace the casual glance by *Sehen*, as Rilke understood it – the lengthy and penetrating observation of everyday reality that gains form in art?

For we are not only media creatures; not all of our experiences, thoughts and emotions are determined by the media. *2030: War Zone Amsterdam* is a revolt against intellectual laziness and indifference, an intense attempt to understand our present-day era and society. As an art historian and curator, I do this with the means that I have – the arts. Paul Virilio presented a plan in

12. Paul Virilio, *Ground Zero* (London: Verso, 2002), 48-51.

2002 for a 'Museum of Accidents' as a response to the avalanche of natural and man-made accidents, mishaps and disasters that we are witnessing today. Although the uniformity of the selected works of art, many of which were literal and familiar images of disasters, made the exhibition less convincing than the accompanying publication, the intention behind it appealed to me greatly. Virilio did not stoically wait until a disaster occurred in his vicinity, he nefariously turned the situation around. Instead of being exposed to accidents, he exposes the accidents in a new kind of museum-science and museography.[13]

13. Paul Virilio, *Unknown Quantity* (London: Thames & Hudson, 2003), the catalogue of the eponymous exhibition in Fondation Cartier pour l'art contemporain, Paris, 29 November 2002 – 20 March 2003.

My exhibition 'Soft Target. War as a Daily, First-Hand Reality' in 2005, with 14 hours of film and video material, installations and paintings, was a protest against the 'shock and awe' spectacle of war in the media. With 'Soft Target', I attempted to avoid putting on a classical exhibition in the white cube of the Basis Actuele Kunst (BAK) institute in Utrecht by using a number of spaces in the Hoog Catharijne shopping mall in addition to those of BAK, with the goal of having a more open relation with the outside world. With *2030: War Zone Amsterdam*, I operate entirely outside the walls of art institutes, in an attempt to go a step further than the symbolic representation of reality in the – oh, so familiar and oh, so safe – environment of museums and art institutes.

Locations, Artists and Communication

The public does not have to pay admission to this event; after all, nobody buys a ticket for war. Short artistic interventions and performances will take place on the squares and streets of the city; the artists will also infiltrate festivals, exhibitions and publications, with or without the knowledge of the organizers. In underground spaces in the city – ranging from cold war bunkers and emergency tunnels to underground brick and concrete tanks for water storage when floods threaten – activities will take place at scheduled times in these 'last' places of refuge in the future war zone of Amsterdam.

All of the 30 participating artists and artist collectives, whom I have met during my travels to the Middle East, Eastern Europe, Canada and within Western Europe over the past one and a half years, have already done projects in public space and know the obstacles of working outside the white cube. Many of these artists, especially those from non-Western countries, are also curators and have organizational experience. In addition to seeking variety in the themes, disciplines and work of the artists, I have also sought to create a fruitful composition of the group as a whole, inviting warmongers as well as peacekeepers, worrywarts as well as optimists. Some of the artists live and work in war zones or former war zones; with their personal experience of war and expertise as artists, they will look at this fictitious assignment differently than will artists who are at home in the Dutch or Western situation. During a week of workshops and explorations when the artists collectively go round the city, a good deal of time will be reserved for discussions with the artists and the project team about the basic assumptions of the event.[14]

The conditions of war will be taken into consideration for all communications. What

14. The project team is comprised of Dyveke Rood (assistant curator), Rimme Rypkema (researcher), Hansje Lo-A-Njoe (logistics and catering), Christiane Bosman (communications) and Rudolf Evenhuis (registration).

is available after all of the familiar media fall away – no Internet, no television, no cell phones? The group will discuss how underground activities can be communicated in such a way that they are difficult to trace and yet reach a large and varied public. For starters, we will look at low-tech examples from art history such as mail art and contemporary sub-cultural expressions like graffiti, but high-tech means of communication will also be investigated. The great mobility of people in the cultural world will be used for making international contacts and spreading news. A number of representatives from the general press will be invited to participate in the event as embedded journalists.

The results of the event are extremely uncertain. Will it remain a theoretical *Spielerei* for the few, or will it truly hold up a mirror to a broad public and get them thinking about their own position in a country that, according to some, is on the verge of civil war, and according to others, has already been in a state of war for some time? As far as I'm concerned, one thing is certain: there are no spectators, everyone is a participant.

Artists 2030: *War Zone Amsterdam*

Maja Bajevic
Sarajevo, 1967/ Paris

Joze Barsi
Ljubljana, 1955

Sawsan Bou Khaled
Beirut, 1975

Persijn Broersen
Margit Lukács
Delft, 1974/ Amsterdam, 1973

Giorgio Andreotta Calò
Venice, 1979/ Amsterdam

Tony Chakar
Beirut, 1968

Lana Čmajčanin
Sarajevo, 1984

Danny Devos
Vilvoorde, 1959/ Antwerp

Katja van Driel
Kleve, 1971/ Amsterdam

Ronen Eidelman
Jaffa, 1971

Jamelie Hassan
London, Ontario, 1948

Khaled Hourani
Ramallah, 1965

IRWIN
Dusan Mandič, Ljubljana, 1954

Miran Mohar, Novo Mesto, 1958

Andrej Savski, Ljubljana,1961

Roman Uranjek, Ljubljana,1961

Borut Vogelnik, Kranj, 1959/ Ljubljana

Adi Kaplan/ Shahar Carmel
Kibutz Ein Hahoresh, 1967/ Tel Aviv, 1958/ Tel Aviv

Nesrine Khodr
Beirut, 1973

Gert Jan Kocken
Ravenstein, 1971/ Amsterdam

Reine Mahfouz
Beirut, 1975

Hwayeon Nam
Seoul, 1979

Pil and Galia Kollectiv
Jerusalem, 1975/1976/ London

PiST///
Didem Özbek, Karabük, 1970

Osman Bozkurt, Karabük, 1970/ Istanbul

Plastique Fantastique
David Burrows, London, 1965

Simon O'Sullivan, Norwich, 1967/ London

Sebastian Romo
Mexico City, 1973

Menachem Roth
Israel, 1975

Eran Sachs
Jerusalem, 1975 / Jaffa

Sala-Manca Group
Lea Mauas, Buenos Aires, 1974

Diego Rotman, Buenos Aires, 1972, Jerusalem

Malkit Shoshan
Haifa, 1976 / Amsterdam

TG42
Joeri Vos, Haren, 1981

Isil Vos, Haren, 1986

Mariana Aparicio Torres, Leiden, 1983

Noel S. Keulen, Heerlen, 1978/ Amsterdam and Rotterdam

Alite Thijsen
Eibergen, 1957/ Amsterdam

Philippe Van Wolputte
Antwerp, 1982 / Amsterdam

Willem Schinkel

The Continuation of the City by Other Means

Now that politics is deliberately being shunted aside with greater and greater frequency and all sorts of measures that sooner apply to an emergency are being legitimized, cities are coming under increasing pressure. War rhetoric and marketing strategies are converging in the formulation of urban policies that are primarily aimed at attracting the creative class and integrating the 'underclass'. Reflecting on Amsterdam's future, sociologist Willem Schinkel reacts to the marketing slogan 'I Amsterdam' by asking, '*Who* is Amsterdam and *where* is it heading?'

A municipal government that wishes to attract the 'creative class' – and this includes practically the entire upper middle class – employs a paradoxical marketing strategy. On the one hand, the city is pictured as a creative space in which innovation, amusement and cultural edification combine to form what is in fact a utopia, a blissful place that does not exist. On the other hand, the city is pictured as a dystopia, a miserable place in which crime, deprivation and all the rest of it have the upper hand, and in which vigorous steps must be taken in order to make and keep the city attractive for the middle class. This place does not exist either, but its image is effective because it mobilizes policy. Those who want to do something about 'the underprivileged districts' must pull open all the semantic registers in order to present the situation as serious, for nothing will happen in Rotterdam Zuid, The Hague Transvaal or Amsterdam Slotervaart for less than millions. The creative class, in turn, has every reason to contribute to the dystopian image of the city because in accordance with the classic pattern of gentrification it can live cheaply where it is a pioneer in the urban jungle.

The ultimate semantic register is that of war. War rhetoric is often heard in contemporary urban policy. There is a 'front line', for example, with 'front-line workers' who need sufficient 'striking power' to carry out 'interventions'. 'Urban recovery' is accomplished in this manner, sometimes even with the aid of so-called 'city marines' or 'housing brigades'.

To properly access the theme of 'Amsterdam at War', I would first of all like to examine the present – and perhaps also future – meaning of the concept of war. Next, I will discuss the role played by the rhetoric of war in the city's political economy, and in that light I will conclude by taking a critical look at the current city marketing campaign – 'I Amsterdam' – by posing the question, 'Who is Amsterdam?'

After the Cold War: Global Warming?

Nowadays, war is increasingly becoming a metaphor. Real wars are usually either civil wars or unequal wars between highly technological armies and highly ideological guerrillas. The era of war between nation-states seems to be largely over. In one respect, this has to do with the scale of potential destruction reached in the twentieth century: a war would not last long enough to be a 'war' or have a winner (which is what was expressed with the ambiguous acronym 'MAD' – Mutually Assured Destruction). This is why the end of the Second World War did not bring peace, but what political commentator Walter Lippmann called a 'Cold War'.[1] Peace became the continuation of war by other means.

1. Walter Lippmann, *The Cold War: A Study in U.S. Foreign Policy* (New York: Harper Row, 1947).

Our present-day world is tending toward a multi-polar division of power in which the Cold War situation remains as relevant as ever. Most of what now passes for war, however, is no longer war as we have known it since modernity. Modernity actually brought order to the wars in the West. After the religious wars in the sixteenth and seventeenth centuries, the Peace of Westphalia (1648) introduced the beginning of a system of inter-state relations that did not so much outlaw war as regulate it. Wars were kept relatively controllable because they were conducted between sovereign nation-states. A typical characteristic of a nation-state was that it could, with sufficient grievances, start a war. This is one of the claims explicitly expressed in the American Declaration of Independence (1776): the right to start a war.[2] The increased interweaving of modern nation-states has meant that wars between two nation-states have grown scarcer. War has been replaced by more diffuse forms of political violence. But the model of war, which in its most 'pure' sense is characterized by political opposition between 'friend' and 'enemy', as the political philosopher Carl Schmitt put it, is on the contrary more alive than ever – albeit, paradoxically enough, in a strongly depoliticized sense.

2. *The Declaration of Independence* (New York: Bantam Books, 1998 [1776]), 58.

War is a metaphor, a rhetoric that has real effects. For example, the USA recently has been able to conduct two 'old-fashioned' wars against nation-states (Afghanistan and Iraq) because it used the rhetoric of war to describe a situation that did not satisfy the characteristics of a war: the War on Terror was a rhetorical recoding of the conflict between the USA and Al-Qaeda terrorists that ultimately could legitimize two wars. But there also have been a 'war on poverty' (Lyndon B. Johnson, 1964) and a 'war on drugs' (Richard Nixon, 1969). Such wars converge in urban policy that is aimed at what was once known as the 'urban crisis'.

Social-Hypochondriacal Management of the Portrayal of the Enemy

The rhetoric of war in fact leads to the transposition of war from 'politics', as Jacques Rancière terms it, to 'police'. He understands 'police' and 'policing' to be the rational management of society, the distribution and legitimization of places and roles. As such, the police is a supplement to politics, the post-political moment of rule that is the necessary medium of politics, whereby politics is understood by Rancière to be that which breaks with the order of the police, the place of that which has no place, the 'part of those who have no part'.[3] Thus arises a rational management of the idea of the enemy, conforming to the police model rather than to the propaganda model. The enemy is not an enemy but a pathological phenomenon that must be 'included'. And it is precisely this attempt at inclusion that causes permanent exclusion, in the sense that it denotes a permanent battleground of urban police. In an era when politics post-ideologically parades ideals that go no further

3. Jacques Rancière, *Disagreement: Politics and Philosophy* (Minneapolis: University of Minnesota Press, 1999), 28-30.

than maintaining economic growth and safeguarding 'liveability' and 'safety', politics is nothing more or less than a legitimizing mechanism (across the entire political spectrum) for the selective pathologization of the urban population – a mechanism that legitimizes through allusion to that urban population, namely through the populist argument of standing up for 'the people in the underprivileged districts'.

The post-political context can be seen as the condition (a weak condition) that I have dubbed 'social hypochondria'.[4] This ties in with a metaphor of corporeality that has been used throughout history to describe social and political life. Like the human body, society, according to the organicistic view, was a whole consisting of parts. An example of such a corporeal representation of society is Plato's image of the polis. At the top, at the head of the social body, was the *logos*: the philosopher-regents. Below that was the noble disposition, the *thymos*, the source of the higher aspirations: the sentinels. And, similar to the human body, Plato saw the lower regions of the social body as the source of the lower aspirations, the *eros*. This was equivalent to ordinary people in the polis.

Nowadays, we have a social concept that still exhibits characteristics of the old corporeal mentality. We think of society as a whole that is comprised of individual parts; we

4. See: Willem Schinkel, *Denken in een tijd van sociale hypochondrie: Aanzet tot een theorie voorbij de maatschappij* (Kampen: Klement, 2007).

are concerned about 'cohesion' and 'integration' – typical corporeal terminology – and we ascribe a top and a bottom to society (for there happens to be such a thing as a 'social ladder'). As with every bottom, the bottom of society is spoken of in a negative fashion. Thus, just as with Plato, the problematizing of the bottom of society is an erotic consideration. The most important erogenous zones of society are at the bottom of the social body. This is why contemporary cultural offensives are a form of moral politics, conceived for the purpose of disciplining the eroticism of the lowest regions to conform to the norms and values of good social mores.

This erotic self-palpitation of the social body is a typical form of social hypochondria. Social hypochondria arises at the moment that the social body no longer is making its way toward a goal, but is stuck with itself. It no longer really believes in Progress or the Last Judgment – on the contrary, it has exposed Progress as the Last Prejudice. It is thus a body with amputated legs, no longer going anywhere and simply sitting still, focused on itself, feeling its body and finding all sorts of complaints and disorders – for which the most common denominator undoubtedly is 'integration'.

Over the past several years, however, 'integration policy' has become increasingly localized, concentrating on the city – and within its borders, on the district or neighbourhood. Like Plato's polis and also later on, as Richard Sennett for instance has shown, today's city is equally often seen as an organism.[5] And nowadays the city is the body upon which semi-military operations are carried out and where the 'front line' of policy is to be found. The trenches of the city's political economy lie in the neighbourhoods characterized by poverty. Here, poverty often goes together with ethnicity, in the sense that people who have a 'non-Western background' are relatively among the poorest and at the same time by far the most important target groups for policies on integration, citizenship, living standards, safety and social cohesion.

5. Richard Sennett, *Flesh and Stone: The Body and the City in Western Civilization* (New York: W.W. Norton, 1994).

One of the most prevalent images of the enemy is accordingly that of the foreigner. The figure of the *hostis*, both guest and enemy,[6] contains in one word what is currently the most important configuration of friend ('society') and enemy (the foreigner who, to use a spatial metaphor, 'stands outside society'). But before the foreigner is conceived of as an enemy within populist rhetoric, city policy latches onto the 'non-integrated' figure, which more broadly speaking can be the 'non-civilized', those who are not adapted to the modern economy: the single mother (often 'Antillean'), the housebound mother (often 'Moroccan'), the adolescent school dropout (usually 'boys').

6. See: Jacques Derrida, *Over gastvrijheid* (Amsterdam: Boom, 1998).

So, in a certain sense there is an enemy, but this is not the enemy that is in diametrical, antagonistic opposition to the friend, such as in the political theory of Carl Schmitt. It is sooner the enemy who simultaneously is a guest – the foreigner who is close enough to be completely included and assimilated,[7] the person who still has to become civilized into an autonomous, tolerant subject. This is a 'suitable enemy',[8] an 'enemy within', to be sure, but mainly threatening because of his or her pathological deviation.

7. Compare: Loïc Wacquant, *Urban Outcasts: A Comparative Sociology of Advanced Marginality* (Cambridge: Polity, 2008).

8. Compare: Loïc Wacquant, 'Suitable Enemies. Foreigners and Immigrants in the Prisons of Europe', in: *Punishment & Society* (1999), 1(2), 215-222.

If war is conducted in the city, what is at stake in the battle at the 'frontline' of city policy is the transformation of *this* enemy. That war is about the erogenous zones of the city, the 'inside outsider's spaces',[9] the 'safety zones' or 'hot spots' that accommodate the 'pit' of the city, the bottom that does not disappear as long as there is also a top and that therefore is in danger of becoming a semi-permanent target of the police.

9. Keith J. Hayward, *City Limits: Crime, Consumer Culture and the Urban Experience* (London: Glasshouse Press, 2004).

War in the City: Not Militarizing but Depoliticizing

As Rancière says, a police that focuses on the management of these groups puts itself in the position of effectuating what is constitutive for democracy: involved citizens, safety, a social bond. This is why politics is not what characterizes the contemporary city. Urban policy, for instance in the sphere of what is fashionably known as 'social cohesion' at the moment, produces what is seen as a condition for politics – a production process that necessarily precedes the political. Here I will leave the utopian hope expressed in Rancière's notion of 'politics' (politics as the antagonistic speaking of those who have no voice) for what it is. I am concerned about the growing dominance of a post-ideological form of population management ('police') that has an increasingly stronger spatial and local character. Michel Foucault, in his lectures at the Collège de France, described how the concept of 'police' in France during the seventeenth to the nineteenth centuries meant something totally different than it does today. It indicated an ensemble of techniques related to various spheres such as public order, municipal hygiene, health, public administration, and so forth. In the most general sense, 'police' and 'policing' was described as the administrative governance of a community.[10] In fact, all of the 'good' use of the state's power was seen as 'policing'.[11] Rancière's notion of 'police' refers back to Foucault's analysis.[12] And when Rancière himself describes policing as 'not so much the "disciplining" of bodies as a rule governing their appearing, a configuration of *occupations* and the properties of the spaces where these occupations are distributed', perhaps this has a still too narrow, economic focus.

10. Michel Foucault, *Sécurité, territoire, population: Cours au Collège de France, 1977-1978* (Paris: Seuil/Gallimard, 2004), 320-321.

11. Ibid., 321.

12. Rancière, *Disagreement*, op. cit (note 3), 28.

The spatial focus is nevertheless evident. Just as in Foucault's analysis, 'policing' concerns a certain milieu of the troubled community. The contemporary concept of 'policing', moreover, is again changing in a way that seems to be coming closer to the earlier concept that Foucault described. Nowadays, 'the' police are responsible for a growing number of functions and have a growing number of functionaries. This is particularly clear in the city. Not only do the police operate from time to time in 'public-private partnerships',[13] but 'civic guards' and citizens are also increasingly being mobilized. Civic guards have been given powers of arrest and citizens are being mobilized to act as what Jane Jacobs called 'eyes on the street',[14] albeit this time as 'eyes of the state' also. Civilians, often with great initiative on their part, are becoming involved as community workers or as 'burghers in blue', complete with (blue) uniforms. In general, the civilian is being 'responsibilized'. The neoliberal emphasis on 'individual responsibility' easily goes together with the conservative-communitarian emphasis on 'community'. This combination, which can be called 'neoliberal communitarianism',[15] is what situates the individual in a milieu that can be managed.

13. For international comparison, see: Trevor Jones and Tim Newburn (eds.) *Plural Policing: A Comparative Perspective* (London: Routledge, 2006).

14. Jane Jacobs, *The Death and Life of Great American Cities* (New York: Vintage, 1961), 35.

15. See: F. van Houdt and W. Schinkel, 'The Double Helix of Cultural Assimilationism and Neoliberalism: Interpreting Recent Transformations of the Concept of Citizenship in the Netherlands'. Forthcoming (2009).

The Continuation of the City by Other Means

Particularly in the area of 'safety', which smoothly transitions into the problematization of 'filth' (such as the 'broken windows' ideology, for example, which in the Netherlands translates as 'clean, intact and safe' and 'neat, orderly and peaceful'), this 'responsibilization' is the furthest advanced.[16] This evolution of 'the' police, however, is simply part of a broader development from politics to police. I would also therefore understand 'policing' to be an entirety of practices and principles that has the spatial management of populations as its object.

The increasing spatial action taken by 'the police' occurs on the basis of techniques that are part of this 'policing': the analysis of 'criminogenic spaces', the actuarial estimation of individual risks on the basis of aggregated data, the 'tackling' of a mixture of 'nuisance and crime' that in fact expands the domain of criminality and thereby strengthens urban dystopia and further fixates it as the object of police control. To an increasing degree, this is all couched in terms of a 'target area approach' within which both an 'individual approach' and a 'group approach' are distinguished on the basis of commercial policy advice. The difference between the last two lies in the size of the targeted milieu (only family or also beyond that). Administrative regulations such as prohibited areas, collective barring from stores and public transport prohibitions also are part of this.

An immediate effect of the creation of such a police is the depoliticization of the relation between the privileged and the nonprivileged. Or, even more fundamentally, a depoliticization of political antagonism per se, a sublimation of a tension that can be called 'the political'.[17] Schmitt also called depoliticization a neutralization of political antagonism, because the 'enemy' is now rationally managed and no longer is on the same plane as the 'friend'.[18] The enemy is 'moralized' and – a purely Kantian thought, paradoxically – 'pathologized'. Scientists who act as 'social pathologists'[19] zoom in on the city and mark out the zones that are 'multi-problematical'. Policymakers march out to intervene behind the front door and in the womb. Evermore intimate spheres – in Sloterdijk's terminology, psychosocial space bubbles or 'autogenic vessels'[20] – are pried open in order to break through pathological discontinuities with the sphere of the statistically normal. The localizable private, the *oikos*, becomes the exclusive focus of a police work that consequently is in danger of not only forgetting the public, the polis,

16. Compare with: David Garland, *The Culture of Control: Crime and Social Order in Contemporary Society* (Chicago: Chicago University Press, 2001).

17. See, for example: Claude Lefort, *Essais sur le politique: XIXᵉ-XXᵉ siècles* (Paris: Seuil, 1986); Sheldon Wolin, *Politics and Vision: Continuity and Innovation in Western Political Thought* (Princeton: Princeton University Press, 2004).

18. Carl Schmitt, 'Das Zeitalter der Neutralisierungen und Entpolitisierungen', *Der Begriff des Politischen* (Berlin: Duncker & Humblot, 2002), 79-95.

19. C. Wright Mills, 'The Professional Ideology of Social Pathologists', in: Irving Louis Horowitz (ed.), *Power, Politics and People: The Collected Essays of C. Wright Mills* (New York: Oxford University Press, 1969), 525-552.

20. See: Peter Sloterdijk, *Sphären I: Blasen* (Frankfurt/M.: Suhrkamp, 1998), 60-61.

but also the critical questioning of fundamental economic distributions. The public sphere is a republican hope that particularly because of the neoliberal communitarian emphasis on 'individual responsibility' and 'civil society' is unmasked as a depoliticizing diversion tactic: since it is *between* market and state, it accepts the position of 'go play your utopian games there', so that neither market nor state are subjected to real criticism. Meanwhile, a silent war is raging on the police front, which with every 'innovative policy intervention' brings further depoliticizing. And the political? That can only come to the fore in grotesquely remodelled questions on 'privacy'.

In the cultural sphere, depoliticizing takes place on the basis of what political scientist Wendy Brown analyses as the idea of 'tolerance' used as a civilizing instrument of power.[21] The identification of what is 'liberal' and 'Western' with tolerance legitimizes an intolerance on the basis of tolerance[22] which is never politically refuted because the speaker would place him or herself outside the order of tolerance. Urban areas where the 'barbarians' (Wendy Brown) reside who do not satisfy the idea of Western – but nonetheless universal – tolerance are 'tackled' with 'zero tolerance' rhetoric. In the economic sphere, depoliticization subsequently takes place by coding the economic (class positions, for example) as the cultural – as 'behavioural codes', 'street culture' or 'culture' alone. This completes the Mobius strip of depoliticization, for the cultural recoding of the economic sphere always brings the administration of the urban population (police, 'policy') back to the opposition between the advanced and the backward, the mobile and the stationary (the 'disadvantaged').

The Exception as the Rule: The City as War Zone?

The militarization of the city has been described by various urban sociologists. Mike Davis, for example, shows how Los Angeles more and more resembles an area 'under siege'. The fear of crime is leading to a 'Fortress LA', which according to Davis entails the destruction of public space.[23] What's more, in a recent book Davis sees the car bomb as the paradigm of the new (urban) warfare.[24] The 'war' that is increasingly characterizing Dutch cities, however, is presumably not a militarized war. It is sooner about the construction of asymmetrical portrayals of the enemy by means of policing. The 'enemy' is thereby managed, both in the sense of 'containment' (the Cold War doctrine) and 'pre-pressure': a prevention that in fact includes the adjustment and repression of undesirable lifestyles.

Why is this police-form of popula-

21. See: Wendy Brown, *Regulating Aversion: Tolerance in the Age of Identity and Empire* (Princeton: Princeton University Press, 2006), 13.

22. Also see: Schinkel, *Denken in een tijd van sociale hypochondrie*, op. cit. (note 4); Willem Schinkel, *De gedroomde samenleving* (Kampen: Klement, 2008).

23. Mike Davis, *City of Quartz: Excavating the Future in Los Angeles* (London: Verso, 1990).

24. Mike Davis, *Buda's Wagon: A Brief History of the Car Bomb* (London: Verso, 2007).

tion control now focusing so strongly on space in general and the city in particular? Because time is no longer an ideological category. The 'big stories' of modern times, not in the least Marxism, were temporalized schemes for future emancipation.[25]

Such narratives have lost overall plausibility and made way for local forms of population management that no longer are characterized by politics but by police. This is why we often hear that 'time is running out'. The only time that matters is the 'now'; there's – literally – no time like the present. As such, modernity achieves its goal, for modernity has always been the only era to describe itself via the *modo*, the 'now'. The new urban state of war is characterized by a rhetoric of moral legitimacy: the problems we have *now* are so appalling that special, even exceptional measures are required. The state of emergency is announced rhetorically. Giorgio Agamben has described how the exceptional case of sovereignty has become the dominant paradigm of contemporary politics.[26] He speaks of a development in which politics is increasingly being sidelined by government. This, says Agamben, leads to the production of what the Romans called the *homo sacer*, the outlaw who is outside the community that is characterized by law. The exception and the *hors la loi* explanation, however, are not the absolute, unadul-

25. See, for example: Edward W. Soja, *Postmodern Geographies: The Reassertion of Space in Critical Social Theory* (London: Verso, 1989)

26. Giorgio Agamben, *Homo Sacer: Sovereign Power and Bare Life* (Stanford: Stanford University Press, 1998).

terated categories that Agamben presupposes. The policing of 'marginals' in the city is more and more often taking the form of the semi-exception, whereby urban zones move in and out of the sphere of the law and subjects gradually are transformed into *homo sacer* for the duration of the implementation of a particular policy instrument.[27] The enclosing exclusion of the *homo sacer* is in reality more diffuse than Agamben suggests.

27. See: Willem Schinkel and Marguerite van den Berg, 'City of Exception. Revanchist Urbanism and the Urban *Homo Sacer*'. Forthcoming (2009).

This generalized state of emergency is precisely what continually sets the definition of the community bound by law (*bíos*) at stake against bare life (*zoè*) enclosed by exclusion. The community is thus in a permanent state of siege. In this situation, a 'cease-fire' would mean the dissolution of the community itself. As the artist/writer Dan Perjovschi noted in New York's MOMA in 2007, global warming is not all that has come after the Cold War. In future, war threatens to become an urban condition, a phase that the city can slip in and out of, an exception that threatens to become the rule.

Conclusion: 'Who Amsterdam' in 2030?

The present slogan for Amsterdam city marketing is 'I Amsterdam'. This perfectly expresses the paradoxical combination of neoliberal communitarianism. On the one hand, there is the narcissistic Cartesian primacy of the 'I' or rather, the 'I Am' implicit in the slogan. This 'I Am' has no other qualitative interpretation than that of a seamless overlap with the city. The 'I Am' is inseparably connected with 'Amsterdam' and therefore indicates that the 'I' can only exist when it conforms to the rules of the city. The organicistic yearning for the seamless overlap between individual and collective is deployed here as a marketing instrument. And like every marketing campaign, it presents the fiction of a seamless overlap that in reality does not exist without friction.

If I may speculate about the state of affairs in 2030: The image of the city conceals a permanent struggle over the criteria for inclusion in the 'marketed' city image. This takes the form of a 'perpetual war', but certainly not in the way that Noam Chomsky envisions. This war – which, like every war in an era of globalization, is a civil war – is not recognized or acknowledged as such because it is conducted in the form of policing, as urban policy aimed at population control. To the extent that it does not scare off tourists, this is perchance conducted with the bellicose rhetoric of urban dystopia, but it is not 'war' in any familiar sense. It is not a fight over the 'ghetto' – which the Netherlands does not have and undoubtedly will not have 20 years from now. The mark of a ghetto is that you cannot leave it; on the contrary, what is problematized as detrimental to the quality of life in city districts is the rapidity with which people move out of them. Amsterdam will more probably have developed new techniques for the spatial fixation of an object by assimilation-oriented police in 2030.

In this sense, it is very well possible that the individual body will play a role through the use of biometric indicators. After all, the outsourcing of politics is coupled with an outsourcing of control over the individual. In terms of specific populations and locations, we will probably see the harnessing of a new form of surveillance – no longer one of panoptic surveillance, but of *selfveillance*, a form of self control in which the body is both the controlling and controlled agency.[28] The iris scan for the frequent flyer at the airport is the cosmopolitan example of this. The equivalent in the battle – which is otherwise invisible for that cosmopolitan – against the degeneration of the urban community is perhaps the implant, which indicates who (meaning poor, ethnic minorities and/or criminal subpopulations) is moving where in the city. This incorporates the state of emergency in biological life, which then on one tramline belongs to the *bíos* of the community, but on another to the *zoè* of bare life, for which some parts of the law are nullified for statistical reasons (deviation from the 'normal population').

'Selfveillance' assembles individuals from 'dividuals'. People are scattered (bit by bit) throughout different control systems as dividuals and are assembled into 'in-dividuals' as soon

28. Willem Schinkel, 'De nieuwe technologieën van de zelfcontrole: van *surveillance* naar *zelfveillance*', in: Marguerite van den Berg, Marcel Ham and Corien Prins (eds.), *In de greep van de technologie: Hoe we kwetsbaarder en onafhankelijker worden* (Amsterdam: Van Gennep, 2008), 171-187.

as an attribution of bare life by such systems (a positive identification as a body-to-be-identified) comes into play. The object of that attribution (for instance the carrier of a self-identifying chip) is a self only insofar as (s)he controls him- or herself. [29] The individual's self is thus affected by the control which it carries out on itself (as recently became clear with the self-control on the Metro turnstile: '(in)eligibility'). The controlled individual produces the control herself, because the control is a signal that leads to a contingent amalgamation of data – in one district this means, for example, that a person is there 'illegally', in the other, not. Such is the urban 'war' that I can envision in the Amsterdam of 2030. The first skirmishes of this invisible battle will become visible on the flip side of the injunction 'I Amsterdam'. For artists, I believe it is a matter of turning against the sublimated creativity of the 'creative class' and of not identifying with the 'I Amsterdam' identification. Art should sooner creatively investigate '*Who, Amsterdam?*' – and also: '*Where are you heading, Amsterdam?*' [30]

29. In 2007, news reports stated that Mexico would give South American migrants who crossed the southern border of Mexico a chip in order to track their movements. In the end, this turned out to be chip cards, not biochips.

30. Compare Peter Sloterdijk, *Sphären I: Blasen* (Frankfurt/M.: Suhrkamp, 1998), 644: 'Wo sind wir, wenn wir im Ungeheuren sind?'

GOOD
NEWS

As of 2010, the price of *Open* will be lowered. From then on, *Open* will cost € 19 50 for the Dutch-language version and € 23 50 for the English-language version.

Subscription rates will also be lowered from € 39 50 to € 32 50 for the Dutch-language version and from € 49 00 to € 39 50 for the English-language version. The subscription rate for students will be € 24 50.

The editors of *Open*, SKOR and NAi Publishers have come to this decision because of the fact that *Open* is acquiring an increasingly higher profile on the international market. We feel it very important that *Open*, published with public funds, remain affordable for everyone interested in the formulation of theories on art and the public domain.

We hope you will continue to read *Open* in the future!

Frank Furedi

Refusing to Perform Fear

In the Netherlands, the politicization and dramatization of fear is preventing people from seeing the real problems, according to sociologist Frank Furedi. It is high time we realize that this in fact has to do with an estrangement from our own identity, especially as it has developed since the 1960s. Furedi thus argues for a more future-oriented activism, in which we must ask ourselves what the Netherlands and Amsterdam in particular want to be in the future.

One of the interesting features of contemporary Western culture is the pervasive character of the discourse of fear. Whether you travel to New York, Berlin or Amsterdam, you are confronted with the *zeitgeist* of fear. To put it starkly, the stories that people tell you in bars, cafes and on the streets are far less about hope than about fear. Unlike hoping, fearing enjoys considerable cultural affirmation. When I arrive in Amsterdam I am soon warned about gangs of pick-pockets. On its website the Tourism Office warns visitors to beware of fake policeman who are out to rob them. Parents tell me that the city streets in the Netherlands are not safe for children anymore. And even friends who feel liberated from these very conventional conformist fears caution me to beware of opportunistic politicians who are out to scare the public with their politics of fear.

Of course the institutionalization of a discourse of fear through the issuing of health warnings, risk management or media alerts should not be interpreted as proof that the quantity of fears has increased. It merely indicates that fear serves as a frame through which we interpret a variety of experiences. Numerous catch phrases – politics of fear, fear of crime, fear of the future, fear factor – are testimony to its significance as a cultural idiom for interpreting experience. The usage or even over-usage of the term indicates that fear is not simply a reaction to a specific danger but a cultural metaphor for inter-

preting life. Politics has internalized this culture of fear. So political disagreements are often over which risk the public should worry about the most. That is why politics in Europe is dominated by debates about the fear of terror, the fear of asylum seekers, the fear of anti-social behaviour and crime, fears over children, fears about our culture, fear for the environment, fear about our health or fear of economic insecurity.

Although opportunist politicians often seek to politicize fear they are not the principal problem. The politics of fear could not flourish if it did not resonate so powerfully with today's cultural climate. Politicians cannot simply create fear from thin air. The reason why the politics of fear has such a powerful resonance is because of the unusually feeble sense of human agency that prevails in twenty-first century Europe. Contemporary society posits the idea that the defining characteristic of humanity is its vulnerability and the idealization of powerlessness that dominates public life.[1] This state of diminished agency disposes people to interpret events through the prism of anxiety and fear. And if vulnerability is indeed the defining feature of the human condition, we are quite entitled to fear everything.

1. See Frank Furedi, *Invitation To Terror; The Expanding Empire of the Unknown* (London: Continuum Press, 2007), chapter 5.

The open advocacy of fear indicates that it has become a cultural metaphor for interpreting and representing the world around us. Indeed, in some circles fear is used as a form of affectation to signify a sensitivity to the many hidden perils facing people. 'I am really worried about my child surfing the Net' parents tell one another to display their parental responsibility. To acknowledge fear is to demonstrate awareness. This self-conscious affectation does not mean that people are necessarily more scared than previously. It merely signals the idea that they ought to be. When one of my Dutch friends informs me that 'Geert Wilders really scares me', she is not simply making a political statement. Her acknowledgment of this fear represents a statement about her identity – she is the kind of person that finds Wilders scary. 'Whom and what we fear, and how we express and act upon our fearing, is in some quite important sense as, Durkheim long ago realized, constitutive of who we are.'[2]

That is why the promotion of fear has important implications for the constitution of identity. Through performing fear we indicate what kind of a person we are. So the acknowledgement of anxiety about the threat represented by Wilders serves to emphasize a psychic distance from those prejudiced and ignorant people who want to turn the clock back to the mythical good old days. Others adopt a different script. They fear that the Netherlands' Enlightenment values are under threat by misguided and dangerous multicultural policies. As far as they are concerned their public avowal of such concerns expresses a

2. R. Sparks, E. Girling and I. Loader, 'Fear and Everyday Urban Lives', *Urban Studies*, nos. 5-6, vol. 38 (2001).

long overdue statement about something that until recently could not be said. That's the kind of people they are.

What distinguishes the Netherlands from many of its neighbours is not its internalization of a culture of fear but a tendency to communicate it in a usually dramatic and caricatured form. The dramatization of fear, particularly in relation to the domain of culture, has acquired a grotesque form among the populist right. Both Pim Fortuyn and Theo van Gogh were consummate performers who sought to dramatize people's existential insecurity through cultivating the media. There is something utterly banal about the attempts of Theo van Gogh and Geert Wilders to produce shocking films. Through embracing the identity of 'I am here to shock and provoke' they went through the motion of producing a twenty-first-century version of an emptied-out medieval passion play. In a more enlightened era such infantile 'crying wolf' stories would remain on the margin of society. But many Dutch people could not resist the temptation to embrace the role of the righteously provoked. And in turn numerous politicians and public figures responded by issuing warnings about the dangerous consequences of showing these films. Their prophecy of a violent reaction by offended minorities can be seen as an invitation to the exercise of fearful protest. Many authors of anti-xenophobe counter narratives profess to be even more shocked than

Ayaan Hirsi Ali and Theo van Gogh with the female lead during the filming of *Submission* (2004). Photo Thomas Kist, © ANP

their populist opponents. If one was to take seriously their assessment of the threat posed by Wilders it would be difficult to avoid the conclusion that the Netherlands is going through a period that strongly resembles the final days of Weimar Germany.

This affectation of fear often signals a fatalistic sensibility towards the world. That is why the statement 'I am scared' is rarely followed by an indication of doing something about the object of fear. Worse still, the dramatization of fear influences our behaviour through encouraging us to be passive and anxious about the future. It promotes cynicism and confusion. It incites us to regard ourselves as victims of circumstances beyond our control instead of authors of our destiny. Instead of responding to chauvinist propaganda by developing a robust humanist progressive alternative, far too many people react by simply asserting their fears. Yet is it is crucial to rebel against the power of the fear entrepreneurs. One step in that direction is to understand the workings of the culture of fear.

Amsterdam's Uncertain Identity

Amsterdam, like most European cities, is not at ease with itself. Despite the fact that it is a relatively safe and secure urban environment, many people in Amsterdam perceive life through the prism of insecurity and fear. In recent years the low-grade fears associated with the management of individual insecurity have often become focused on concerns about cultural and community identity. It seems that since its inception, the War on Terror has had a greater cultural impact on the Netherlands than other Western societies. One illustration of this trend is the growth of public apprehension towards the Muslim presence in the country. A study carried out by Pew Global Attitudes suggests that the Netherlands is one of the most anti-Islamic countries in Europe, where a majority of the people view Muslims unfavourably. Unfavourable attitudes towards Muslims or immigrants are often symbolic of a more fundamental sense of disorientation about the world. Public attitudes towards immigrants are often shaped by concerns to do with cultural and community identity. Such sentiments are underpinned by concerns about cultural security and values. That's why it is not surprising that anxieties about the integration of immigrants into Dutch society coincide with growing disenchantment with the EU.[3]

3. See for example L. McLaren, 'Anti-Immigrant Prejudice in Europe: Contact, Threat Perception, and Prefrences for the Exclusion of Migrants', *Social Forces*, no.3, vol. 81 (2003).

One of the inevitable consequences of the War on Terror was to raise questions about what defined Western culture and society. Former President Bush raised this issue poignantly when he asked 'Why Do They Hate Us'? The very posing of this question conveyed a sense of surprise and bewilderment. It also expresses frustration and distress about the fact that not everyone loves us. When this question was originally formulated it was based on the premise that 'they' came from somewhere very far away. The threat posed by people that 'hated us' was conceptualized as being external to Western societies. However, since 9/11 it has become increasingly difficult to ignore the fact that this threat is not just an external but also a domestic problem. And the realization that there are many young Muslims living in the Netherlands who do not like their society, do not want to be like us and maybe even hate us gives this threat an all-too-intimate status. Through the discovery and construction of home-grown Islamic radicalization, the Netherlands has found a tangible focus for deliberating on its elusive identity.

'We were flabbergasted to learn that she had become a fanatic,' noted a teacher of Bouchra El-Hor, a young Dutch Moroccan mother who was charged in Britain with a terrorist offence. According to her teacher she was a 'normal Dutch girl'. Reports indicated that she 'looked like an immigrant success story' and hung out at the pub with her friends and was known for her fashionable taste in clothes.[4] The realization that she did not want to be 'a normal Dutch girl' coincides with an almost panic-like discovery that a significant section of the population is estranged from its society. Instead of posing the obvious question of why Dutch society lacked a capacity

4. See Craig Whitlock, 'Terrorists Proving Harder to Profile', *The Washington Post*, 12 March 2007.

to culturally integrate its population, many public figures opted for the strategy of politicizing immigration and integration. Through this process uncertainties about Dutch identity were recast as a threat posed by unassimilated and dangerous minorities. One of the regrettable consequences of the dramatization of cultural fears is that it serves as an invitation to counter performance. The traumatic legacy of the murder of Theo van Gogh serves as a reminder that individual acts of violence can have spectacular effects.

However, it is not so much the lure of radicalism as the unravelling of the meaning of being Dutch that is responsible for the sudden rise of the politics of fear in the country. To some extent the political class has contributed to this state of affairs by first pursuing a narrow technocratic approach towards immigration before panicking and politicizing the issue. In a sense their politics of fear has little in common with a traditional Machiavellian plot. It represents a performance that signals the idea that you can trust us because we are taking firm steps to deal with this problem. This new tough approach, like the previous technocratic one, by-passes the problem of answering the question of what binds society together. As an outsider I am continually struck by the theatrical quality of the Dutch debate on issues such as identity, culture, immigration and integration. Am I a little prejudiced when I tell myself that only disoriented Dutch politicians could have dreamt up the idea of producing the video *Coming to the Netherlands* for prospective migrants? The video purports to inform migrants of Dutch life through scenes that include nudity and homosexuality. Is this what it means to be Dutch?

Nowhere else in the world would policymakers dream up the idea of making prospective migrants sit through *Coming to the Netherlands*. The very manner in which Dutchness is presented – liberal, tolerant, permissive – suggests that what is at issue is not the nation's historic past and traditions but the values and ethos that have emerged since the 1960s. It is worth noting that until the 1960s Dutch society was strongly influenced by a relatively conservative and religious ethos. The 1960s saw a dramatic rupture with this tradition and gradually the Dutch cultural elites began to perceive themselves as not simply tolerant, but also permissive. In the Netherlands and throughout the world Amsterdam has come to symbolize this cosmopolitan, secular and permissive consensus. Arguably that is why so many otherwise liberally minded people have developed a degree of cultural hostility towards a politicized Islam. It is not simply a question of Islam representing a threat to Dutch culture – more importantly it is experienced as a threat to individual lifestyles and identities. It is not simply that 'they are not like us', but also the question of 'Why don't they let us be ourselves?'. So Amsterdam does not simply suffer from an identity crisis but also from lifestyle related ones.

Refusing to Perform Fear

When threatened identities become politicized they have a nasty tendency to invite a collective mood of insecurity and vulnerability. But once people become aware of the fact that the fundamental problem is not 'them' but their estrangement from their identity it becomes possible to confront the city's insecurities. The question that needs to be posed is what kind of a community does Amsterdam want to be in the future. Through transcending the petty questions of lifestyle identity politics, people can begin to consider real alternatives. A more future-oriented activism is the precondition for freeing ourselves from the fatalistic imagination that assigns people the status of powerlessness. Fortunately, the story of Amsterdam cannot be reduced to a tale of threatened identities. It is a place where individual anxieties coexist with the aspiration for solidarity and gaining meaning from experience. Despite perceptions of cultural threats many people know that they need to be open-minded and are ready to yield to new experience. What they need is a language through which they express their desire to be subjects rather than objects of change.

The response of a community to a threat and its level of morale is influenced by its shared experience and values and the meaning attached to

Dear reader,

SUB
SCR
IBE!

open

I wish to subscribe to *open*

Subscriptions (2 issues per year)
Within Europe €39.50 / Outside Europe €45.00 /
Students €24.50. Postage included.

Name ....

Initial(s) .... M/F ....

Address ....

....

Postcode / Zip Code .... City ....

Country ....

Telephone ....

E-mail ....

Number on student ID card ....

Signature .... Date ....

NAi Publishers
Int. Business
Reply Service
IBRS/CCRI No 5025
3000 VB Rotterdam
The Netherlands

them. It is through a grown-up public deliberation on the meaning of its shared experience that Amsterdam can develop its potential for dealing with the challenges it faces.

The human imagination possesses a formidable capacity to engage and learn from the risks it faces. Throughout history humanity has learnt from its setbacks and losses and has developed ways of systematically identifying, evaluating, selecting and implementing options for dealing with threats. There is always an alternative. We can renounce the distinct human qualities that have helped to transform and humanize the world and resign ourselves to the culture of fatalism that prevails today. Or we can do the opposite. Instead of celebrating passivity and vulnerability we can set about humanizing our existence. Instead of becoming an audience for yet another spectacle of fear we can take over the stage and refuse to yield to the scaremongers.

Bryan Finoki

The City in the Crosshairs

A Conversation with Stephen Graham

The investigations of geographer
and writer Stephen Graham show
us a city not only caught in
the crosshairs of a perpetual war
between international military
coalitions and their swarming
counterparts, but a city that's
been reframed, re-imaged, as
a strategic site in a larger geoeconomic scheme for engineering
the urban machinations of control
that are necessary to secure the
triumph of neoliberal capitalism
across the globe.

BRYAN FINOKI To begin, I am wondering how you conceptualize the Global City and its military role in expanding global capital. I am also interested in the opposite notion, of how cities can be inherently resistant to imperialism rather than acting as mere pistons for the expansion of capitalist development.

STEPHEN GRAHAM Global cities, as the key nodes in the transnational architectures of neoliberal capitalism, are vitally important militarily. They organize the financialization and production of space (London, for example, basically controls the financial architectures of large swathes of Africa and the Middle East). They orchestrate the extending dominance of neoliberalism. They serve as key hubs in the lacing of the world through transnational control, transport and logistics infrastructures. And they are, of course, preeminent symbolic spaces for transnational capitalism, making them vulnerable as symbolic targets.

But, as you say, global cities, like all cities, are porous and mixed up spaces, and amount to an infinite variety of space-times way beyond those of the financial core, the logistics function, or the power of the state. The diasporic communities and social movements that are most actively contesting neoliberal capitalism all work through, and within, what geographer Peter Taylor has called, the *World City Network*. This is the idea that it is an integrated network of world or global cities that orchestrates the geographies and political economies of neoliberal capitalism.[1]

1. See GaWC: Globalization and World Cities. Online at http://www.lboro.ac.uk/gawc/.

BF And, of course, with a network of global cities comes a corresponding expansion of militarism. Much of your work deconstructs the ways and processes that militarism has become increasingly blurred in the heightened security of the Western city. How does this domestic militarization of space mirror that occurring in the bombastic urban sprawl of the underdeveloped world? Aren't both of these geographies exhibiting more and more similar urban complexions that would suggest no place in this century is exempt from being readied for war?

SG I think so. The global mixing in today's world renders any simple dualism between North and South, or Developed and

Developing, very unhelpful. Instead, it's more useful to think of transnational architectures of control, wealth and power, as passing through and inhabiting all of these zones but in a wide variety of ways. Extreme poverty exists in many 'developed cities' while enclaves of supermodern and high-tech wealth pepper the cities on South East, Southern and Eastern Asia.

Militarized geographies of (attempted) control are fully inscribed into the construction, maintenance and extension of these archipelago geographies. Take, for example, the militarized borders and surveillance systems which organize the relationship between foreign, 'free' trade and export processing zones and the 'outside'. Or the relationship between gated communities, privatized public plazas, 'security' zones or airports, and the 'normal' city 'outside'. In all these cases we see the emergence of new urban borders where control architectures and technologies are used to try and force the flows of the city through 'obligatory passage points' where they can be scrutinized and, if possible, identified.

> BF Even though perhaps these 'obligatory passage points' have always been a part of capital's fabric and are now just fulfilling their role at a time of hyper-urbanization and migration through an embedded pattern of urban bordering, I feel like we have entered the age of the checkpoint, both symbolically with the mechanisms monitoring the global flows of capital but also literally with the proliferation of military checkpoints.
>
> Which sort of leads me to my next question: I'm fascinated by how your work traces a spatial narrative of conflict and the morphology of the city as a kind of fossilization of political violence over time. Could you enlighten us with a brief history of the city in the context of violence?

SG The histories of the city and of political violence are, of course, inseparably linked. As Lewis Mumford teaches us, security is, of course, one of the very reasons for the very origins of urbanization. The evolution of urban morphology, as you say, is closely connected to the evolution of the geographies and technologies of war and political violence: fortification and the bounding of urban space through defensive and aggressive architecture are especially central to this long and complex story. So, too, is the fortification of cities to the symbolic demonstration of wealth, power and aggression, and as the commercial demarcation of territorialities. The elaborate histories of siege craft, atrocity, the symbolic sacking and erasure of urban space, and cat and mouse interplay of tactics and strategies of attack and tactics and strategies of defence, are all central here. Much of the Old Testament, in fact, is made up of fables of attempted and successful urban annihilation. As Marshall Berman has argued: 'Myths of urban ruin grow at our culture's root.' Important, here, are the symbolic roles of urban sites as icons of victory, domination and political or religious regime change.

All of this is fairly obvious. What fascinates me is that the histories of modern and late capitalist urban development tend to retreat from and obfuscate the continued centrality of cities as strategic sites within war and political violence. The obvious, physical, architectures of fortification have clearly left the city as it becomes 'over-exposed' – in Virilio's terms – to the new optics and technics of transnational and Total War. Remaining fortifications, at that point, are re-inscribed as tourist sites: reminders of a simple relationship between architecture and violence. And – at least until recently – nation-states have clearly worked to construct and maintain their monopolies on political violence in a way that rendered cities as mere targets. This reached its apogee within the Cold War imaginaries of full-scale nuclear Armageddon.

Partly because of these changes, the more stealthy and subtle relationships between modern urbanism and war, when discussed at all, now lurk more in the interstices of urban debate. Who recalls the obsession of CIAM and Le Corbusier's Ville Radieuse with building 'towers in the park' not just as generators of a new machinic urbanism, or of the interplay of light and air, but as buildings that were both difficult to hit through aerial bombing and which would raise their inhabitants up above expected aerial gas attacks? Who remembers the role of nuclear paranoia in adding further momentum to the racialized politics of 'White Flight' in the USA during the 1950s? And who, in their architecture or planning training, are treated to courses on the roles of these disciplines as engines of destruction, annihilation and politicized violence against those people and places deemed to be anti-modern, backward, unclean, or dangerous to the state, or the fetishized image of the emergent 'global' city?

These obfuscations mean that architecture and critical urbanism remain ill-equipped to deal with the way in which war and political violence are re-entering the city in the post-Cold War world.

BF Is it a general lack of awareness in academia and other fields of urban practice that prevents understanding these very types of repercussions inherent to the practice of the built environment? Or, is it emblematic of a deeper pervasive ignorance among architects and planners that don't care to understand how the intrinsic political nature of their work may serve to hasten the racialization of the landscape, or the negative pathological effects of frenzied securitization? I mean, is it just a blatant refusal on the part of urban practitioners today to have a political conscience?

SG Architects and urban planners are often still wedded to a heroic and positive self-image where their efforts necessarily work to render the world a better place. Construction and regeneration are the watch words: the inevitable destruction, erasure and political violence involved are obfuscated or taboo. This is linked to a poor understanding of the politics of urban space and their roles within projects of militarism and political violence.

Critical theorists Ryan Bishop and Gregory Clancey recently suggested that modern urban social science in general has shown marked tendencies since the Second World War to directly avoid tropes of catastrophism (especially in the West). They argue that this is because the complete annihilation of urban places conflicted with its underlying, enlightenment-tinged notions of progress, order and modernization. In the post-war, Cold War, period, especially, 'The City', they write, had a 'heroic status in both capitalist and socialist storytelling'. This worked against an analysis of the city as a scene of catastrophic death. 'The city-as-target' remained, therefore, 'a reading long buried under layers of academic Modernism'.

Bishop and Clancey also believe that this 'absence of death within The City also reflected the larger economy of death within the academy: its studied absence from some disciplines [urban social science] and compensatory over-compensation in others [history]'. In disciplinary terms, the result of this was that the 'urban' tended to remain hermetically separated from the 'strategic'. 'Military' issues were carefully demarcated from 'civil' ones. And the overwhelmingly 'local' concerns of modern urban social science were kept rigidly apart from (inter)national ones. This left urban social science to address the local, civil, and domestic rather than the (inter)national, the military or the strategic. Such concerns were the preserve of history, as well as the fast-emerging disciplines of international politics and international relations. In the dominant hubs of English-speaking urban social science – North America and the UK – these two intellectual worlds virtually never crossed, separated as they were by disciplinary boundaries, scalar orientations and theoretical traditions.[2]

2. See Ryan Bishop and Gregory Clancey, 'The City as Target, or Perpetuation and Death', in: R. Bishop, J. Phillips and W.W. Yeo (eds.), *Postcolonial Urbanism* (New York: Routledge, 2003), 63-86.

BF Also, it seems the military itself is the quickest to make use of the connections between war and space, or even architecture theory, not only as a means for better strategizing their campaigns of urbicide and creative destruction, but perhaps also as a way to gain further legitimacy for their planning – hijacking the discourse of architectural urban theory to bolster the technical approvals of their surgical destruction of the built environment, no?

SG While Israeli military theorists have appropriated Deleuze and Guattari (see Eyal Weizman's new book *Hollow Land*), most of the US military material about cities looks more like a high school urban geography class. (Even in Israel, this approach is now out of favour).

The level of debate here is very simplistic and recycles old stereotypes from Orientalist urban books like Spiro Kostof's *City Assembled* (for instance, Islamic cities have no real structure, etcetera). As far as I can see, there is a strong disconnect between the more theoretical treatments of military transformation and the challenges of 'urban operations'.

BF Is the type of defensive urbanism we see today that attempts to bomb proof our skyscrapers and wall off different enclaves in Baghdad merely a new iteration of an ancient strategy to fortify sovereignty – a postmodern medievalism, if you will – or have we reached a completely new definition of 'military urbanism'? How do you distinguish 'military urbanism' from 'new' military urbanism?

SG The 'postmodern medievalism' is a fascinating argument,
I think. There is certainly a sense among military theorists of
scrambling to look back at the proxy urban wars of colonialism
– and elsewhere – to learn lessons that might help inform tactics
in places like Baghdad.

However, I don't think we really are going 'back to the future'
in some simplistic way. Rather, political violence and war are
being re-inscribed into the micro-geographies and architectures of cities in ways that, while superficially similar to historic
defensive urbanism, inevitably reflect contemporary conditions.
Important here, at the very least, are some points of distinction:

– The constant real-time transmission of video, images and text
  via TV and the Internet;
– The increasingly seamless merging between security, corrections, surveillance, military and entertainment industries who
  work continually to supply, generate, fetishize and profit from
  urban targeting, war and securitization;
– A proliferating range of private, public and private-public
  bodies legitimized to act violently on behalf of capital, the
  state, or 'the international system';
– The mass and repeated simulacral participation of citizens
  within spaces of digitized war, especially Orientalized video
  games produced by the military;
– The particular vulnerabilities of contemporary capitalist cities
  to the disruption or appropriation of the technical systems
  on which urban life relies. (These are caused by the prolifera-
  tion, extension and acceleration of all manner of mobilities,
  the tight space-time coupling of the technical infrastructural
  flows that sustain 'globalization', and, more prosaically, the
  fact that modern urbanites have few if any alternatives when
  the fuel stops, the electricity is down, the water ceases, or the
  food and communication stops; or the waste is not removed);
– The ways in which borders and bordering technologies are
  emerging as global assemblages continually linking sensors,
  databases, defensive and security architectures and the
  scanning of bodies;
– The centrality of 'urbicidal' violence or neglect to the new
  geographies of 'primitive accumulation' through which private
  military corporations and 'reconstruction coalitions' produce,
  and benefit from 'disaster capitalism' (Naomi Klein's term) or
  'accumulation by dispossession' (David Harvey's phrase) –
  whether in Baghdad or New Orleans; and

- The growing importance of roaming circuits of temporary securitized zones, set up and policed by cosmopolitan roaming armies of specialists, to encompass G8 summits, Olympics, World Cups, and so forth.

Added to this, we have new relationships emerging in the long-standing interplay of social and urban control experiments practiced on the populations of colonized cities and lands, and appropriated back by states and elites to develop architectures of control in the cities at the 'heart of empire'. Thus, biometric borders emerge around Fallujah before being inscribed into the world's airline systems. The complex legal and architectural geographies of extra-territoriality, permanent exception, and privatized political violence are set out through the global system of establishing and securitizing off-shore trading and manufacturing enclaves before being implanted into the Palestine territories or the War on Terror's 'archipelago of enclaves'. The Israeli practice to 'shoot on sight' is directly imitated, following advice from the IDF, by UK counter-terrorist operations on the London tube after 7/7. And the Pentagon's experiments in the tracking of entire urban traffic systems provide an input into the shift to 'smart' or 'algorithmic' CCTV in Western cities.

All these connections, of course, are lubricated by the fact that it is the same corporate bodies that are driving forward both the new strategies of urban warfare in the Middle East and the 'surveillance surge' as part of the Homeland Security's drive in the global North.

BF And I think that gets at the biggest important distinction between then and now. That is, the sheer capitalist industrial-complex nature of the defence economy that doesn't just fortify the city to protect it from violence and war, but the global-scale arming of nations and geoeconomic restructuring of conflict zones that insure conflict will always exist, in order to profit off of the modern defensive measures that go into regulating these conflict zones. What do you think?

SG I completely agree: these complexes don't just celebrate and fetishize war and wholesale securitization – they need it. The deepening crossovers between war industries and policing, event management, border control, urban security and entertainment work to permeate and normalize cultures of war and militarism in a way where traditional separations between the 'inside' of nations and the 'outside' increasingly fall away.

BF I know you have a new book you are working on (or a couple of new books actually), one of which is entitled Cities Under Siege. Could you tell us about that and how it departs from your previous work in your book *Cities, War, and Terrorism*?

SG *Cities Under Siege: The New Military Urbanism* will be a sole-authored book, published through a non-academic press (Verso), rather than, as with *Cities, War, and Terrorism*, an edited, academic text. I hope, therefore, to make it more coherent and accessible to the proverbial 'lay' audience that Verso can reach.

The book aims to expose the complex processes and politics through which Western military doctrine is increasingly preoccupied with the micro-geographies, architectures and cultures of urban sites. In this sense, it is a further attempt in my effort to develop an explicitly urban rendition of critical geopolitical analysis that commenced within *Cities, War, and Terrorism*.

The main body of *Cities Under Siege* will raise a key set of dimensions to the urban 'turn' within Western military doctrine, thinking and practice. It will address the powerful anti-urban imaginative geographies which tend to essentialize cities as Hobbesian sites of decay, hyper-violence and threats to political establishments. The book will also link this to a discussion of how ideologies of 'battlespace' within contemporary military doctrine – whether it be the *Revolution in Military Affairs* (RMA), 'asymmetric warfare', the ideas of 'effects-based operations' and 'fourth generation warfare', or the Pentagon's new obsession with the 'Long War' – which essentially amounts to the rendering of all terrain as a persistently militarized zone without limits of time and space. The other five chapters in the book will explore: the technophiliac dreams of omniscience and total surveillance that are so powerful within US military discourse about cities; the ways in which state militaries like the USA and Israel routinely target essential urban infrastructures; the role of digital play and physical urban simulation within the 'media-industrial-military-entertainment' network; the importance of fantasies of erasing particular places through urbicidal warfare'; and the relationship between war and the increasingly milita-rized design and semiotics of automobiles.

BF Wow, that sounds fascinating. What can I say, I can't wait. I'm reminded of the work of Philipp Misselwitz and Tim Rieniets who in a recent book, City of Collision, describe 'conflict urbanism' as a diagnosis of Jerusalem and the types of flexible spatial configurations that have produced, in their words, 'a city in a permanent state of destruction and reinvention, hostage to political planning, collective fear and physical and mental walls'. But, clearly this speaks more widely about the urban transformations that are happening in regions all over (as it sounds like Cities Under Siege also gets at) including the capitalist sanctums of the Northern hemisphere.

How has the military always exercized both a direct and indirect role in the urban design of cities? How can we gage the relationship between urban planners and military strategists today in the transformation of the contemporary Western city?

SG The Israeli experience, in terms of reorganizing the architectures of control in the colonized West Bank, launching permanent and 'pre-emptive' military strikes against Palestinian and other cities, and in the intense securitizing of its own cities, is clearly the paradigmatic case of contemporary military urbanism. So, the constantly morphing geographies of Jerusalem, Gaza and the West Bank, as important studies by people like Eyal Weizman, Philipp Misselwitz and Tim Rieniets have demonstrated, are vitally important.

But these cases are much more than mere paradigmatic examples: they are exemplars that are being actively imitated and exported around the world. To a large degree, Israel's economy is now a service-security economy that relies very much on selling its products, weapons and what we might call 'military urbanism services' to all comers. The shooting of the Brazilian Jean Charles de Menezes on the London Underground on 22 July 2005 was the result of a direct imitation of Israeli 'shoot to kill' policy against suspected suicide bombers. The USA's use of biometric borders, targeted assassinations, and D9 caterpillar bulldozers in Iraq were all directly brought in from Israel. And US forces are working very closely with the Israeli military in undertaking their own urban warfare and training doctrine.

Regarding the military in exercising a direct or indirect role in the urban design of cities, the role has more often been

The City in the Crosshairs   43

indirect than direct. But a key trend now is for the US military to become much more actively involved within 'urban operations' in US cities, a trend which undermines the rulings of the Posse Comitatus Act of 1878, which was designed to inhibit military operations within the continental USA. Now, US forces have a strategic command for North America (Northcom). They regularly undertake urban warfare exercises and simulations in real US cities, and they are increasingly blurring with the more militarized ends of the law enforcement agencies, creating a military-civil continuum rather than a binary separation. It is this continuum that directs the shaping of security zones, new checkpoints, and other defensive architectures in US cities, along with major inputs from building regulation changes. This is happening along with important participation from architects, landscape architects, geographers, planners and urban designers on the contemporary challenges of urban securitization. Added to this, though, are major coalitions of commercial actors such as insurance, real estate bodies, and what the ACLU has called the 'Surveillance Industrial Complex'. Also involved are transnational players like the organizers of major sporting events and political meetings who are keen to use each event as roaming experiments in state-of-the-art urban securitization.

BF In a previous article of yours, 'From Space to Street Corners: Global South Cities and US Military Technophilia', you talk about how Western post-Cold War military analysis has depicted the processes of urbanization in the global South as 'essentialized spaces' which are meant to undermine the high-technology of US military power. Partially because Western strategists had neglected urban warfare throughout the Cold War in favour of a heavy reliance on the Air Force, which had to essentialize another projection about 'enemy space', where cities weren't battlefields but rather large scale targets – treating the battle space as object, if you will. But, I'm hoping you could further explain how the process of urbanization in the global South is being recharacterized by the West in such a way that has allowed the US military to retool their doctrine for greater technomilitarism and its use in guerrilla warfare. Is it fair to say that the poor cities of the world are being re-imaged by the west specifically to justify a shift in military strategy and to legitimate a 'Long War'?

SG This is certainly a very important shift. Along with the portrayal of the 'internal colonies' of inner urban cores in US or UK cities, or the Parisian *banlieus*, as Hobbesian spaces housing the dangerous, racialized other, military and security discourses about global South cities depict such places as essentialized, Hobbesian places of anarchy. One influential article by Richard Norton, for example, calls such places 'feral cities' which threaten the global capitalist order because they house massive populations, create social and political unrest, are often not governed in any formal sense, and provide breeding grounds for extreme ideologies. Fear of 'failed cities' thus seems to be even more powerful than fear of 'failed states'.

A key writer in this vein is *New York Times* columnist and self-styled urban warfare commentator Ralph Peters.[3] Peters' military mind recoils in horror at the prospect of US forces habitually fighting in the majority of the world's burgeoning megacities and urbanizing corridors. To him, these are spaces where 'human waste goes undisposed, the air is appalling, and mankind is rotting'.[4] Here cities and urbanization represent decay, anarchy, disorder and the post-Cold War collapse of 'failed' nation-states. 'Boom cities pay for failed states, post-modern dispersed cities pay for failed states, and failed cities turn into killing grounds and reservoirs for humanity's surplus and discards (guess where we will fight).'[5]

3. See Ralph Peters, 'Our Soldiers, Their Cities', *Parameters*, spring 1996, 1-7; and Ralph Peters, 'The Future of Armored Warfare', *Parameters*, autumn 1997, 1-9.

4. Peters, 'Our Soldiers', op. cit. (note 3), 2.

5. Ibid., 3.

Peters highlights the key geostrategic role of urban regions within the post-Cold War period starkly: 'Who cares about Upper Egypt if Cairo is calm? We do not deal with Indonesia – we deal with Jakarta. In our [then] recent evacuation of Sierra Leone Freetown was all that mattered.'[6] Peters also candidly characterizes the role of the US military within the emerging neoliberal 'empire' with the USA as the central military enforcer (although he obviously doesn't use these words, coined by Hardt and Negri). 'Our future military expeditions will increasingly defend our foreign investments,' he writes, 'rather than defending [the home nation] against foreign invasions. And we will fight to subdue anarchy and violent "isms" because disorder is bad for business. All of this activity will focus on cities.'

6. Peters, 'The Future of Armored Warfare', op. cit. (note 3), 5.

Again, in synchrony with his colleagues, Peters sees the deliberate exploitation of urban terrain by opponents of US hegemony to be a key likely feature of future war. Here, high-tech military dominance is assumed to directly fuel the urbanization of resistance. 'The long term trend in open-area combat is toward overhead dominance by U.S. forces,' he observes.[7] 'Battlefield awareness may prove so complete, and "precision" weapons so widely-available and effective, that enemy ground-based combat systems will not be able to survive in the deserts, plains, and fields that have seen so many of history's main battles.' As a result, he argues that the USA's 'enemies will be forced into cities and other complex terrain, such as industrial developments and inter-city sprawl'.[8]

7. Peters, 'Our Soldiers', op. cit. (note 3), 6.

8. Peters, 'The Future of Armored Warfare', op. cit. (note 3), 4.

To Peters, and many other US military commentators, then, it is as though global urbanization is a dastardly plan to thwart the US military from gaining the full benefit of the complex, expensive and high-tech weapons that the military-industrial complex has spent so many decades piecing together. Annoyingly, cities, as physical objects, simply get in the way of the US military's technophiliac fantasies of trans-global, real-time omnipotence. The fact that 'urbanized terrain' is the product of complex economic, demographic, social and cultural shifts that involve the transformation of whole societies seems to have escaped their gaze.

The supposed geographies of 'feral' global-South cities certainly loom large in the imaginative geographies sustaining Western military doctrine for urban areas. The physical and electronic simulations being produced by Western militaries to train their forces are increasingly including 'garbage dumps, shanty towns, industrial districts, airports' and subterranean infrastructures.

The key thing about Western military operations in global-South cities is that they force military groundedness in militaries that are much more comfortable trying to dictate things from the air using superior sensing and firepower. In Baghdad, high-tech Western surveillance and targeting have not allowed US forces to triumph over determined insurgents utilizing very basic and old-fashioned weapons and guerrilla tactics. Instead, US forces have had to go out on patrol through city streets. This has brought them into very close proximity with insurgents, who have been able to deploy ambushes, improvised explosive devices and rocket-propelled grenades to devastating effect.

A major response from the US military-industrial complex is

to try and reorganize the high-tech and technophiliac weapons and surveillance systems so expensively built up since the last days of the Cold War so that they directly address the needs to 'situational awareness' within the complex, 3d geographies of global-South cities. Programmes with telling titles such as 'Combat Zones That See' and 'Visibuilding' promise to re-establish the dream of omniscient, distanciated and machinic vision for US forces in cities, allowing them to once again withdraw physically from the killing power of their machines. Many dreams of robotised and automated high-tech warfare, permanently projecting perfect power into global south cities, are emerging here. The objective being to try and delegate the decision to kill to computer software embedded within networked weapons and sensors which permanently loiter within or above urban space automatically dispatching those deemed the 'enemy'.

Take, for example, the thoughts of Gordon Johnson, the 'Unmanned Effects' team leader for the US Army's 'Project Alpha' – an organization developing ground robots which respond automatically to gunfire in a city. If such a system can get within one metre, he says, '[it kills] the person who's firing. So, essentially, what we're saying is that anyone who would shoot at our forces would die. Before he can drop that weapon and run, he's probably already dead. Well now, these cowards in Baghdad would have to play with blood and guts every time they shoot at one of our folks. The costs of poker went up significantly . . . The enemy, are they going to give up blood and guts to kill machines? I'm guessing not.'

An even more fetishistic technophiliac fantasy of perfect power emanates from *Defense Watch* magazine, in an article that appeared in 2004 in response to DARPA's announcement that they were developing large-scale computerized video systems to continuously track car movements in entire cities. 'Several large fans are stationed outside the city limits of an urban target that our [sic] guys need to take,' they begin: 'Upon appropriate signal, what appears like a dust cloud emanates from each fan. The cloud is blown into town where it quickly dissipates. After a few minutes of processing by laptop-size processors, a squadron of small, disposable aircraft ascends over the city. The little drones dive into selected areas determined by the initial analysis of data transmitted by the fan-propelled swarm. Where they disperse their nano-payloads.' The scenario continues:

'After this, the processors get even more busy, within minutes the mobile tactical center have a detailed visual and audio picture of every street and building in the entire city. Every hostile [person] has been identified and located. From this point on, nobody in the city moves without the full and complete knowledge of the mobile tactical center. As blind spots are discovered, they can quickly be covered by additional dispersal of more nano-devices. Unmanned air and ground vehicles can now be vectored directly to selected targets to take them out, one by one. Those enemy combatants clever enough to evade actually being taken out by the unmanned units can then be captured or killed by human elements who are guided directly to their locations, with full and complete knowledge of their individual fortifications and defenses . . . When the dust settles on competitive bidding for BAA 03-15 [the code number for the 'Combat Zones That See' programme], and after the first proto- types are delivered several years from now, our guys are in for a mind-boggling treat at the expense of the bad guys.'

> BF Needless to say, the military urbanism of today is clearly less about walls and traditional fortifications (even though we have hardly stopped building them), but really about an entire logic of a production of space and an artificial intelligent system for organizing and policing that space; one designed for control; urban space as a completely new medium that is conducive to contemporary warfare. But, just as much, it seems this new spatial dimension of the War on Terror has also turned the city into a medium for insurgency – what does this suggest about the perceived enemy who is now no longer outside the gates, but also hiding within?

SG As with so much of urban life, the key now is the seamless merging of systems of electronic tracking, tagging, surveillance and targeting into the architectonic and geographical struc- tures of cities and systems of cities. The production of space within the War on Terror thus mobilizes an intensified deploy- ment of these sensors and systems – through global biometric passports, global port management systems, global e-commerce systems, global airline profiling systems and global navigation and targeting systems – within and through the securitizing fabric of urban places. This is very much a Deleuzian and rhizo- matic process which helps to sustain the breaking down of the traditional binary of 'inside/outside' for nation-states and instead brings urban and sociotechnical architectures of security into a range of globe-spanning and telescoping assemblages which continually perform urban life.

BF In addition to the global span of these surveillance technologies, there is also a rampant boom in border fence construction today following, ironically enough, the fall of the Berlin Wall. Not that these wall projects aren't pushing the technological implications of peripheral national security, but I was curious of your assessment of the future of nationalism given this patterning of geopolitical border relations?

SG Certainly architectures of control – architectonic and digital combined – are being mobilized with unprecedented scale in defence of national territoriality. But I think many of these projects are as much symbolic as practical. They are physical demonstrations that nation-states can control global flows of people, goods and capital when, in many cases, this is simply not the case. So the future of nationalism will rely fundamentally on the degree to which it can move away from the idea of an imagined and homogenous community and, instead, come to terms with radical heterogeneity, especially in global cities. If it does not do this, we will see accelerating tensions between ideas sustaining urban governance and those sustaining national governance. For one thing, European nations and Japan, especially, will have no choice but to radically extend their immigration levels if they want to avoid the economic meltdown that will come with geographic ageing.

BF Getting back to an earlier question, I read that the earliest forms of cities were built on forms of conflict and barricading against the natural elements. That is to say, at their root, cities are defined by a defensive kind of urban DNA, I mean – shelter, for all intents and purposes – could be construed as a primitive form of military urbanism. But, clearly we have come a long way towards full-scale gated communities now; what are the psychopathological implications of this morphology? Having moved from improvising mere shelter from the elements to complete enclave barriers against more abstract notions of fear, I guess my question is: How is the culture of an 'Us' and a 'Them', or the 'Other' not only embodied in the current trend of security urbanism, but extensions of an ongoing pathological development?

SG There is a major contradiction here. One the one hand, the Bush doctrine has simplistically relied on the constant invocation of a putative 'us' and 'we' marshalled against a threatening, monster-like, racialized and demonic 'them' who offer an existential threat to 'our' civilization and all its hallmarks ('freedom', 'democracy', and so forth). Here we see long-standing Orientalist tropes being recycled.

On the other hand, it is clear that, in many ways, the cosy, folkish language of 'homeland security' fits very poorly with the transitional cultural, social, ethic and economic realities of US metropolitan regions. So there is a major tension between the construction of an imaginative geography of nationhood as 'us' and the reality of a US metropolitan region. I think this is caused by the fact that it is largely the white exurban USA that forms the real heartland of the republicans: the central cities are as alien, demonized and 'Othered' to them as are Fallujah and Baghdad. So their War on Terror can be thought of as a war against cities both in their own nation and in the colonized war zones. At home this has involved a 'cracking down on Diaspora', in Andrew Shryock's words.

Once again, then, Western nations and transnational blocs – and the securitized cities now seen once again to sit hierarchically within their dominant territorial patronage – are being normatively imagined as bounded, organized spaces with closely controlled, and filtered, relationships with the supposed terrors ready to destroy them at any instant from the 'outside' world. In the USA, for example, national immigration, border control, transportation, and social policy strategies have been remodelled since 9/11 in what Hyndman calls an: 'Attempt to reconstitute the [USA] as a bounded area that can be fortified against outsiders and other global influences. In this imagining of nation, the US ceases to be a constellation of local, national, international, and global relations, experiences, and meanings that coalesce in places like New York City and Washington DC; rather, it is increasingly defined by a 'security perimeter' and the strict surveillance of borders.'[9]

9. See Jennifer Hyndman, 'Beyond Either/Or: A Feminist Analysis of September 11th', *ACME: An International E-Journal for Critical Geographies* (February 2006).

To architect Deborah Natsios, meanwhile, the 'homeland' discourse 'invokes both moral order' and specifically normalizes suburban rather than central-metropolitan urban conditions. The very term 'homeland security', in fact, serves to rework the imaginative geographies of contemporary US urbanism in important ways. It shifts the emphasis away from the complex and mobile diasporic social formations that sustain large metropolitan areas through complex transnational connections, towards a much clearer mapping that implies more identifiable and essentialized geographies of entitlement and threat. This occurs at many scales – from bodies in neighbourhoods, through cities and nations to the transnational – and delineates a separation that works to inscribe definitions of those citizens who are deemed to warrant value and the full protection of citizenship, and those that have been deemed threatening as real or potential sources of 'terrorism': in essence, the targets for the blossoming national security state.

Amy Kaplan argues that the very word 'homeland' itself suggests some 'inexorable connection to a place deeply rooted in the past'. It necessarily problematizes the complex and multiple diasporas that actually constitute the social fabric of contemporary US urbanism. Such language, she suggests, offers a 'folksy rural quality, which combines a German romantic notion of the folk with the heartland of America to resurrect the rural myth of American identity'. At the same time, Kaplan argues that it precludes 'an urban vision of America as multiple turfs with contested points of view and conflicting grounds upon which to stand'.[10]

10. See Amy Kaplan, 'Homeland Insecurities: Reflections on Language and Space', *Radical History Review*, no. 85 (2003), 82-93.

Such a discourse is particularly problematic in 'global' cities like New York, constituted as they are by massive and unknowably complex constellations of diasporic social groups tied intimately into the international (and interurban) divisions of labour that sustain neoliberal capitalism. 'In what sense,' asks Kaplan, 'would New Yorkers refer to their city as the homeland? Home, yes, but homeland? Not likely.' Ironically, even the grim casualty lists of 9/11 revealed the impossibility of separating some purportedly pure, 'inside', or 'homeland city', from the wider international flows and connections that now constitute global cities like New York – even with massive state surveillance and violence. At least 44 nationalities were represented on that list. Many of these were 'illegal' residents in New York City. It follows that, 'if it existed, any comfortable distinction between domestic and international, here and there, us and them, ceased to have meaning after that day'. As Tim Watson writes: 'Global labor migration patterns have . . . brought the world to lower Manhattan to service the corporate office blocks: the dishwashers, messengers, coffee-cart vendors, and office cleaners were Mexican, Bangladeshi, Jamaican and Palestinian. One of the tragedies of September 11th 2001 was that it took such an extraordinary event to reveal the everyday reality of life at the heart of the global city.'[11]

11. See Tim Watson, 'Introduction: Critical Infrastructures after 9/11', *Postcolonial Studies*, no. 6, 109-111.

Posthumously, however, mainstream US media has overwhelmingly represented the dead from 9/11 as though they were a relatively homogeneous body of patriotic US nationals. The cosmopolitanism of the dead has, increasingly, been obscured amid the shrill, nationalist discourses and imaginative geographies of war. The complex ethnic geographies of a pre-eminently 'global city' – as revealed in this grizzly snap-shot – have thus faded from view since Hyndman and Watson wrote those words. The deep social and cultural connections between US cities and the cities in the Middle East that quickly emerged as the prime targets for US military and surveillance power after 9/11, have, similarly, been rendered largely invisible. In short, New York's transnational urbanism, revealed so starkly by the bodies of the dead after 9/11, seems to have submerged beneath the overwhelming and revivified power of nationally-oriented state, military and media discourses.

This interview was conducted on 6 August 2007 for *Subtopia: A Field Guide to Military Urbanism*, and published at: http://subtopia. blogspot.com/2007/08/city-in-crosshairs-conversation-with.html. A second interview followed a month later and can be found at http://subtopia.blogspot. com/2007/09/city-in-crosshairs-conversation-with.html.

Bianca Stigter

Musing Map

An introduction to the art contribution to this issue by Gert Jan
Kocken, which is included as a
loose supplement titled *Depictions of
Amsterdam in the Second World War*.

On 15 May 1940, German soldiers of the 39th Army Corps entered Amsterdam over the Berlage Bridge. Photographs of that entrance have been preserved. In one of them, you can see a map of Amsterdam. A municipal civil servant is standing with it in front of the City Hall on the Oudezijds Voorburgwal. It is a large map, wider than two men and half as high. At the top are two little strings, as if it has just been taken down from the wall. The map was being offered to the German commander so that he could familiarize his troops with the city. A map as a gift — as if the city had rolled onto its back like a dog, saying: go ahead; here are my canals and squares, my hospitals and churches, my barracks and offices, my water and land. Take them.

Nowadays such a gift would no longer be necessary; Google Earth reveals much more than a map of Amsterdam at 1:10,000. In addition to the Internet, we have tom-tom and a company like kaartopmaat.nl. I quote their website: 'As a municipal civil servant, you know how important it is for your city to be accurately mapped out. Literally. Not only for yourself, but especially for the residents of your city. We will gladly help you create a folding map that is precisely tailored to the demands of *your* city. You can — if you wish — make certain information on your city map stand out extra strongly. For example, all of the government agencies, other public buildings such as libraries and theatres, garbage collection district boundaries, public transportation routes, etcetera. You can also show the opening hours of City Hall, important telephone numbers and websites on your map. The municipal coat of arms? No problem. Whatever you want!'

Whether it was necessary back then is debatable. Amsterdam was not terra incognita in 1940. *Fall Gelb*, as the oft-postponed invasion of the Netherlands and Belgium was called, had an *Oberquartiermeister*. The German army had its own maps of the Netherlands at the scales of 1:50,000 and 1:25,000. And naturally, Dutch maps of Amsterdam could simply be purchased. The Germans took advantage of their bridgehead in the city to quarter their troops. On 17 May, the *Ortskommandantur*, the local command, moved into the German Consulate on Museumplein, the building in which the American Consulate is now located.

Today's map of the centre of Amsterdam resembles the 1940 map of the centre of Amsterdam. The half-moon of the canal belt is still the same, the Jordaan area is still the Jordaan, the royal palace still stands on the Dam. Unlike Rotterdam or Arnhem, Amsterdam survived the war relatively unscathed, outwardly. The city was bombed only a few times. Nor did much construction go on during the five years of occupation. Perhaps that's what is so amazing: the 'decor' was already there and it's still there now. Anne Frank's hiding place on the Prinsengracht, the Achterhuis (The Annex), was built in 1740. Today, you cannot tell by looking at it that the volunteer auxiliary police were headquartered in the first public business school on Raamplein in 1942, that there was an eating place in the Derde Weteringdwarsstraat for members of the Dutch Resistance's Reen courier service during the Hunger Winter, that Willemsparkweg 186 was the regional headquarters of the youth branch of the National Socialist Movement in the Netherlands. To name just a few.

You can no longer tell by looking at it, neither at today's reality nor at the map of what was once reality. Yet historical maps can give you an impression of what was important at the time. Here's another quote from kaartopmaat.nl, where they introduce the concept of the *mijmerkaart* or 'musing map': 'A historical map of your city, region or province is truly a "musing map", a voyage of discovery into the past that will give your business contacts great viewing pleasure. A splendid, original and lasting promotional gift.'

During the Second World War, quite a lot of maps were made or re-worked that provided other than the usual information. 'No problem. Everything's possible.' This also seems to have been the mantra of the wartime mapmakers. The most notorious example is the *stippenkaart*, the 'dot map'. In 1941, the Municipal Bureau of Statistics put dots on the map of Amsterdam, with each dot representing ten Jews. On another map, the zealous public servants indicated the distribution of Jews per neighbourhood by colour. The redder the district, the more Jews lived there — until 1943, by which time Jews had vanished from the streets, as Böhmker, the 'Beauftragte of the Reichskommissars for the City of Amsterdam' described the Holocaust. Members of the SD, the German intelligence service, or other Germans occupied the houses of deported Jews located in the better neighbourhoods. The houses in the old Jewish quarter mostly remained empty. In the Hunger Winter, they were ransacked again, this time by people searching for wood to stoke their emergency stoves. Most of these houses were not rebuilt. There, the original decor is gone. In order to gain a picture of the damage, the Municipal Development Company had the ruins charted on a map of Amsterdam, which afterward was nicknamed the *gatenkaart* or 'gap map'.

The Germans also continued to make military maps of Amsterdam and the surrounding area. 'Not for Public View' is still written on these maps in German. In 1943, the Germans began getting ready to defend the city against the expected Allied invasion. Amsterdam was labelled a *Festen Platz*, a city that must be defended to the last bullet. Explosives were put in the dikes. Meanwhile, various resistance groups made maps of the locations of German military bases in the city. Groep Albrecht made an entire album of detailed maps showing all of the schools, garages and barracks that were occupied by the Germans in 1943.

In early 1945, the Dutch Resistance worked out plans for protecting Amsterdam against destruction and armed raids as the German army retreated. The plans included the defence of important facilities such as gas factories and electricity generating stations. The Resistance also charted such things as German telephone lines. Much of this information was collected for the benefit of the Allied forces in England. On some of the maps drawn up by the Resistance, we do not know exactly what is indicated — the red squares and stripes no longer reveal their secrets.

Hanging on a wall in the *Ortskommandantur* on Museumplein was a map of Germany, on which the German military coloured in red the areas of the Reich that the Allies occupied. By May, there were no more white spots.

Artist Gert Jan Kocken spread 33 different maps of Amsterdam across one another in an attempt to give an overall picture of the history of the city: not only the dispersion of Jews but also the location of bombs that did not explode, not only the Germans' military defences but also the attempts made by the resistance to map them. A map is never the place itself, but it almost seems that way on this 'musing map'. Handwritten texts, corrections, sometimes barely legible scribbles, give the maps a materiality that brings the past very close. Even a spot or a scratch is part of this, even these things indicate how people lived and died in Amsterdam. Kocken's map is so large that such details stand out: it measures 310 x 400 cm.

I quote for the last time from kaartopmaat.nl: 'In the beginning of the twenty-first century, we can look at the whole world on our computers, for instance with Google Earth. What has not changed throughout the centuries, however, is the human fascination with maps. When you study a map, you jump into in its landscape, as it were. You search a map for strange, exotic lands and regions. With a bird's-eye view, you trek across high mountains and plains. You follow the endlessly meandering river to its source. Before you know it, the map has you in its grip and hours have passed.'

Replace the landscape with the city, the exotic with the nearby. High mountains are canals, the plain is Museumplein, the Amstel meanders.

This article is partly based on Bianca Stigter's De bezette stad: Plattegrond van Amsterdam 1940-1945 *(Amsterdam: Athenaeum Polak & Van Gennep Publishers, 2005).*

This photograph was taken right after the German troops entered
Amsterdam on 15 May 1940 as they approached the City Hall on
the Oudezijds Voorburgwal. A city official is offering a map of
the city to the German commander. Photo from the Beeldbank W02
archives of the Netherlands Institute for War Documentation

Dirk van Weelden

Letter from Amsterdam

Dear Gerry,

Thank you for your kind e-mail messages and the package with delicious things that you sent us. Please forgive me for being so slow and not answering by e-mail, but it's better for me to send you this letter on paper through our own people. My work for the armed resistance makes it too dangerous to use electronic post for personal messages. I would not be able to write freely.

To start with the best news: Laura and I are healthy, our things are safe in an as yet undamaged warehouse in the Westelijk Havengebied and our house in the Rivierenbuurt is intact. We live in an area where there is still hardly any fighting and where the regime so far has displayed little enthusiasm for purging it. Perhaps this has to do with the Second World War, when so many Jews were deported from this neighbourhood. It would raise too many bad memories.

Like I said, we cleared out most of our valuable possessions, like the books, Ma's grand piano, Laura's jewellery, the silverware and the art and have stashed them safely away. It's much too dangerous to have all that stuff in the house; we live in our apartment with the feeling that we can flee any day, if necessary, with an overnight bag with some clothes and a toothbrush. The bags are packed and ready to go, under the coat rack in the hall.

Many people in Amsterdam are taking advantage of the chaos caused by the civil war for their own ill purposes. In Buitenveldert, bands suddenly started going around and chasing people out of their houses, looting the premises and, after a few blows here and there and a gang rape or two, moving on again. Minibuses towing furniture trailers drove along with them at a footpace in order to carry off the booty. Sometimes they set fire to the houses, sometimes not. When they didn't, it turned out they had made an agreement with the so-called 'Restoration Agents', usually collaborationist notaries, who redistribute the houses of public enemies at the order of the regime. As a matter of fact, most of the addresses the plunderers went to were on a list that the new Minister of the Interior had sent to the Chief of Police of Amsterdam-Amstelland. That's why there's been so little uproar and why the police are only symbolically working on the case. They have plenty of excuses for not having any time. They were called in to maintain order behind the advancing troops when the battle over the Zuidas suddenly broke out and were also requisitioned for Amsterdam East, after the Marines revolted.

I read that a resistance group in Amsterdam North is considering a disciplinary campaign against a band that is causing automobile accidents on the A10 ring road in order to rob the victims. It's discouraging to see how similar those plans are to the emergency legislation that the regime is enacting against us.

Ever since the tourists have been staying away and most of the ex-pats have left, there is a miserable feeling of boredom in the city. As if even the daylight is murky and dim. New ads only appear on the squares and the large thoroughfares. In the rest of the city, the sales, models and packaging are from a year or two ago. The photos are wrinkled by the rain that has seeped into the glass cases. The bright colours are faded, the hairdos of the models looked dated. The world in which those posters belong no longer exists.

The city does not maintain its status any more; there is hardly any upkeep. Even the woodwork on the luxury stores in the Nine Streets is peeling. And all of this is extra noticeable because the streets are so empty – and because a third of the shops have gone bust by now or are open just a few days a week.

In the outdoor cafés, you see only young Amsterdammers, who probably sit there in order to keep an eye on the street for their organization or to make a deal. Even the alleys next to the busier streets and canals are piled with garbage. Even the municipal workers don't like to go in them anymore. Three of the four safe houses that we have in the inner city are on such alleyways. When I walk into an alley it's as if the hand of a giant has picked me up and transported me back in time. For a moment, I'm in the years of the city's degeneracy, the late 1970s, early '80s. I talked to an old journalist who can hardly believe his own conclusion that Amsterdam has been more devastated in a year and a half than in the 150 years prior to that.

As everyone knows, the least chance of explosions, attacks and murders is on and around the Max Euweplein. The casino on that square is one of the most important economic hotspots in the city. Gambling is much more popular than ever - I think because most of the other pleasures have fallen away. But it's also the presence of large amounts of black money and the clandestine business and trading that is done around the casino that gives the Max Euweplein the function of a city centre. This is where the bigwigs of the regime are seen when they are in the city. Elsewhere in the city they don't feel at ease, but in this enclave of louche bling bling and swindle they feel at home.

The regime boasts that it is safe and peaceful around the Leidseplein and the Max Euweplein. But are the volunteers patrolling in their nationalistic uniforms and the heavily armed soldiers with their armoured vehicles on the Weteringschans and the Babylon complex also the boss? Since the introduction of the permit system for journalists, it's not easy to find out who's in charge here, but my impression is that it's primarily the businessmen from all sorts of countries who come to the city in the wake of the ambassador of the friendly Italian regime. They, and the crews of the companies they hire to do the dirty work. The local underworld and the boys and girls of neighbourhood gangs that deal in guns and drugs make up the rest of it. Besides broken English and Amsterdam patois you mostly hear Italian, Serbo-Croatian and Bulgarian.

In the cafés around the Max Euweplein you can also find the foreign journalists, with their differing theories about the source of the money that the regime has at its disposal. Oddly, tax revenues have collapsed but the funds available to the armed forces apparently are inexhaustible.

I am regularly at the Max Euweplein because I also meet with an editor of my London publisher there. I give him USB sticks with stories and essays that I write in English. It's roundabout, but I don't want to risk sending my pieces by Internet. What's more, I publish under a pseudonym. Sometimes one of them gets published and then Jeff, my editor, can give me the money I earn from it – in cash, which is a welcome addition to the little that Laura and I make. As you know, she works as a cook. I'm now an employee at a large dry cleaner's.

Do you remember Harold? That big boorish guy who had a gallery on the Lijnbaansgracht. I think you had hanging on the long wall of your living room. Anyway, this week he suddenly appeared in the dry cleaner's, bringing a pair of trousers, a jacket, suit and a couple of skirts. He looked unhealthy. Red eyes, puffy. He said that besides the gallery he was doing something much more lucrative: selling valuable watches. My not exactly enthusiastic reaction must have shown him I was irritated by the umpteenth bragging story of somebody who is trying to profit from the war. I quickly began to talk about his wife, who was a social worker and probably suffering a lot under the new regime.

Harold burst out in raw, mirthless laughter. She had been interned, and after being interrogated was released. She did lose her job, however. The service at which she worked was located in a 'black district' and declared unnecessary. In the very next breath, he went on to complain about the vigilante groups who were opposing the regime. Why didn't they let the government make a clean sweep, then the repression would automatically lessen and everything could be like it used to be. Living in prosperity, peace and harmony. A provocation. He was not at all surprised to find me working in a dry cleaner's. So he had known all along that I had been fired from the university.

'Harold,' I said, 'little people like you and me have to sit tight and wait it out, try to save our own necks and take care of our loved ones and only join in the discussion again when the madness is over.'

He slammed the money against the counter with his broad, swollen paw.

'Play-actor,' he growled and I gave him the stapled together tickets with a vague smile.

The trains are running again, as I'm sure you've heard. Here you immediately notice it on the street. There are people with maps in their hands walking around again.

The shopkeepers are happy about these courageous visitors. Usually they are people looking up their families or coming to do business.

It took months after the bombardment of the Marine Establishment and the devastation of the Eastern Islands in Amsterdam, but now it's once again possible to travel to the south and east of the country by train. The revolt of the Marines and the Marine Intelligence Service headquartered there did give us hope. Luckily, they were clever enough to smuggle out most of the weapons and vital technical systems before openly turning against the regime. We have already had contact with a few of their commanders and they have a couple of bases near the Rai and in Amsterdam North. I expect a lot from working together with them and who knows, maybe they will succeed in persuading other branches of the armed forces to choose our side.

The evacuation and total destruction of the districts neighbouring the Marine bulwark was a typical example of the misbegotten enthusiasm of the regime. Just ask the Kattenburgers camping in the tents in the Vliegenbos Park whether they consider punishing rebellious marines important enough to blast their houses to bits.

With typical bombast, the regime offered the people from Wittenburg, Kattenburg and Oostburg new apartments on Java Island. After all, plenty of apartments would be freed up after the intellectuals who have been singled out as 'enemies of freedom' or 'agents of Islamo-fascism' were arrested. But then the troops of the regime would have to pacify Java Island first. If it's up to us, that will never succeed. What's more, there are far too many people without a roof over their head.

Yesterday, our group was involved in an over-water attack on the Silodam on the river IJ. There's a company in that building that does research for the regime into the antecedents of subversive activities on the Internet. No security or defences could be discerned, probably because they assumed that no one knew about their freelance work for the AIVD. Our intelligence is very good; we even have moles in the Ministry.

We came from three different directions in canoes painted black with powerful and silent – because they were electric – outboard motors. From less than thirty meters away, we shot two RPGs into the building and lobbed a big phosphor grenade after it to cause an extremely hot fire and thus maximum damage. Our canoes vanished just as quickly in three different directions. No telephonic, radiographic communication had been necessary to plan and carry out the attack. A successful operation, with a quick exit and no traces left.

This was not a solo action by our group. We worked with the Fighting Designers, a group of radicalized designers who seldom engage in armed conflict, by the way, but who lately, especially after the destruction of the eastern islands, Oostelijkeilanden, recognize the necessity to also sabotage the regime by physical means. They provided a skipper, the camouflage clothing and treated the hulls of the canoes so that they are quieter in the water and do not reflect light. I was one of the skippers, and one of the marksmen was ours; we also supplied the canoes. The rocket launchers and the other members of the six-man special commando came from the Amsterdam branch of the Turkish communist party.

The water police and the army still have found no answer to our speedy canoes. We were able to sail into the Haarlemmervaart unhindered and under the cover of darkness reach our hiding place in the Bretten district.

Every week in Café Oostoever, a splendid white concrete 1950s café that overlooks the waters of the Sloterplas in an area that is firmly in the hands of anti-regime militias, I join a think tank of people who discuss peace. We don't talk about how and when peace will come. Meetings about that are held in other places. We consider the problems and possibilities for the city once the regime has been beaten.

One of the leading figures is Bas G., an architect and urban designer. Right before the civil war broke out, he had built his own house on IJburg, and after that island was purged (from which he had a lucky escape) he can only come to the suburbs in the West via secret routes and with false identity papers. He leads an apparently unsuspicious life as a town hall employee who records the city's housing situation. I admire the sangfroid with which he looks at the ticklishness of his daily life from the point of view of the long term. We protect him and his family, but we do this in exchange for information that is valuable for combating and sabotaging the regime.

He always claims that the civil war will turn out to be such a horrible trauma for the Dutch that they will rise above themselves trying to rid themselves of the memory. 'It will better here than it ever was before,' he says nonchalantly, 'not necessarily wealthier, but more lively, international, inventive. In some sectors, such as software, sustainable technology, engineering, we can become world leaders. The difference will lie in rediscovering sharpness and fighting spirit. There will be something to prove. The feeling that we now have of standing with our backs against the wall and seeing everything go to pot will soon give us tremendous energy. A whole lot of crap will disappear like snow under the sun.'

When he talks about the future it calms me down. That's necessary, because the situation can make me desperate. After all, I am participating in the fight against the regime without having an explicit ideology. My loved ones and I are outlawed, considered suspicious and designated as enemies of the people. I was fired and spied upon like a criminal on probation. The reaction was instinctive and intense. I joined a group that is primarily engaged in sabotage, but sometimes also with armed combat.

I am not always completely convinced of the rightness of what we are doing, in the service of which all those terrible things occur, the attacks, the raids, the fires. Hasn't it been true for some time that there are not only two, but four, or maybe even six, parties confronting each other in this mess? A month ago, jihadists from Amsterdam West blew up two commanders of The True Patriots from the Pijp district and bragged about it to boot. Left a gigantic crater on the Fredriksplein. And last week I heard the rumour that the raid on the Social Security office in Amsterdam North was given away by a splinter faction of a Jewish action group. Doesn't this seem more like a war between mafia organizations than a fight for liberation?

How do I know, for example, where the money that pays for our group is coming from? Sometimes we have Israeli weapons, at other times American, but also Belgian and Italian ones. It's also never been completely clear to me how much influence our cell's discussions have on the organization's choices of targets and times. Often I have the impression that they couldn't care less about what we say or think. It could be that behind the organization is an Italian real estate investor who wants to buy a certain section of the city, whether it be for a good price or even destroyed and thus ripe for development.

Laura says at such moments that I should drink herbal tea and get more sleep. Every now and then I think about disappearing to Germany, where it's still a little bit civilized. But those thoughts don't often occur to me after I've spent an evening in Café Oostoever. Bas is able to convince me to stay despite everything. Amsterdam is such a special city in his stories that I want to stay here and fight for it.

This week I was in one of the high-rises in the Zuidas district. The air above the city is different than it used to be. Actually you always see a fire smouldering in a few places in your view. Trails of smoke ranging from dirty yellow to deep black. The difference is even greater when you look down at the city. The bust up roads, the destroyed housing blocks, the roadblocks. The picturesque look and hip international atmosphere is gone, but you do see a tough, sturdy urban structure that can't be messed with that easily. When I looked down at the battered city of Amsterdam I know for sure that we will drive the regime out.

Every day I ride to work on my scooter and pass no less than 18 roadblocks. At ten of them at the least, I am stopped and searched. The weird thing is that I can drive from my house to the Vijzelgracht without a problem, whereas the Rivierenbuurt actually is not occupied by any faction at all at the moment. The centre is indeed in the hands of the regime, but I know for sure that three resistance groups have important bases there. And sometimes we simply make a hit, like when we killed four advisors, among them the great leader's speechwriter, who had gone to a discount computer shop on the Koningsplein. The doors suddenly closed and our people came in from the back garden. The three bodyguards were much too late. Burly farm boys in the big city, they had been gaming.

When I go to see Steef and Ben in the Transvaal neighbourhood, I have to take a detour via the Ceintuurbaan and the Wibautstraat because the Berlage Bridge has been blown up. That was inescapable when we took the Amstel Station, where there were a few trains loaded with weapons and ammunition. Otherwise we would have been attacked from the rear.

But anyway, what I wanted to say is that despite all the havoc and the look of the battlefield, that's the direction I take when I tootle along on my scooter to Steef and Ben on the Steve Bikoplein. They stop me 15 times on this route too, but I look too nondescript, and apparently the profession I once practiced, the history of science, is not suspicious enough to earmark me as an 'intellectual opposed to liberty'.

Gerry, the situation is wretched and disastrous, as you can see, but we haven't had to eat the cats yet and the chance of a blanket bombardment is zilch. If nutters break into the laboratories of the VU and the UvA in order to commit biological terrorist attacks with a couple of test tubes, I'm out of here. Or if the regime lines up its tanks in the Rijnstraat and opens fire on the houses. But I don't see that happening very soon as yet.

Keep your chin up there in Wierden. As far as I know it's a fairly comfortable area to be in during these years of national catastrophe. I'm glad you are there. Say hello to Leo and the children. If you want to send something from the garden again, we would be very grateful. And finally, what's most important of all, thanks for offering to take us in, if life becomes impossible here. I am well aware of how big a risk that is for you. For what it's worth, dear sister, I would do the same for you and yours. Let's hope that it will never be necessary. If it becomes unacceptably dangerous for me here, you will receive a message from our people that we are coming. For now, I am trying to stay here in the city as long as possible. It's terrible to have to say it, but never have I loved Amsterdam as much as I do now, when the city is partly in ruins, ripped up by bulldozers and tanks, mutilated by roadblocks and torn apart by factions shooting at each other.

Hugs from your brother Koos

and from Laura

Open 2009/No.18/2030: *War Zone Amsterdam/Letter from Amsterdam*

Eyal Weizman

Lethal Theory

Architect and researcher Eyal Weizman uses interviews with two brigadier generals of the Israeli Armed Forces, Aviv Kokhavi and Shimon Naveh, the latter of whom headed up the Institute for Operational Theory and Research that closed in 2006, and is now retired, to illustrate the importance of the formulation of theories in the Israeli army's recent ways of conducting a municipal war. He likewise shows what radical and disastrous consequences the 'operational theory' derived from thinkers such as Tschumi, Deleuze and Guattari has for the population.

'I have long, indeed for years, played with the idea of setting out the sphere of life – bios – graphically on a map. First I envisaged an ordinary map, but now I would incline to a general staff's map of a city centre, if such a thing existed. Doubtless it does not, because of the ignorance of the theatre of future wars.'[1]

Walter Benjamin

1. Walter Benjamin, *One-Way Street and Other Writings*, translated by Edmund Jephcott and Kingsley Shorter (London/New York: Verso, 1979), 295.

The manoeuvre conducted by units of the Israeli Defense Forces [IDF] in Nablus in April 2002 was described by its commander, Brigadier General Aviv Kokhavi,[2] as 'inverse geometry', which he explained as 'the re-organization of the urban syntax by means of a series of micro-tactical actions'.[3] During the battle, soldiers moved within the city across 100-m-long 'over-ground-tunnels' carved out of a dense and contiguous urban structure. Although several thousands of soldiers and several hundred Palestinian guerrilla fighters were manoeuvring simultaneously in the city, they were so 'saturated' within its fabric that very few would have been visible from an aerial perspective at any given moment. Furthermore, soldiers used none of the streets, roads, alleys or courtyards that constitute the syntax of the city, and none of the external doors, internal stairwells and windows that constitute the order of buildings, but rather moved horizontally through party walls, and vertically through holes blasted in ceilings and floors.[4] This form of movement, described by the military as 'infestation', sought to redefine inside as outside, and domestic interiors as thoroughfares. Rather than submit to the authority of conventional spatial boundaries and logic, movement became constitutive of space. The three-dimensional progression through walls, ceilings and floors across the urban mass reinterpreted, short-circuited and recomposed both architectural and urban syntax. The IDF's strategy of 'walking-through-walls' involved a conception of the city as not just the site, but the very *medium* of warfare – a flexible, almost liquid medium that is forever contingent and in flux.

At stake are the underlying concepts, assumptions and principles that determine military strategies and tactics. The vast 'intellectual field' that geographer Stephen Graham has called an international 'shadow world' of military urban research institutes and training

2. Kokhavi was the commander of the IDF operation for the evacuation of settlements in the Gaza Strip.

3. Quoted in Hannan Greenberg, 'The Limited Conflict: This is How you Trick Terrorists,' in: *Yediot Aharonot*; www.ynet.co.il (23 March 2004).

4. In fact, after serving their original purpose, the openings forced through the walls immediately become part of the syntax of the city and cannot be reused.

centres that have been established to rethink military operations in cities could be understood as somewhat similar to the international matrix of elite academies of architecture. However, according to urban theorist Simon Marvin, the military-architectural 'shadow world' is currently generating more intense and well-funded urban research programmes than all these university programmes put together, and is certainly aware of the avant-garde urban research conducted in architecture institutions, especially as regards Third World and particularly African cities.[5] Interesting is the fact that there is a considerable overlap among the theoretical texts considered 'essential' by military academies and schools of architecture. Indeed, the reading lists of contemporary military institutions include works from around 1968 (with a special emphasis on the writings of Deleuze, Guattari and Debord), as well as more contemporary writings on urbanism, psychology, cybernetics and postcolonial and poststructuralist theory. If writers claiming that the space for criticality has to some extent withered away in late twentieth-century capitalist culture are right, it surely seems to have found a place to flourish in the military.

5. Simon Marvin, 'Military Urban Research Programmes: Normalising the Remote Control of Cities', paper delivered to the conference, 'Cities as Strategic Sites: Militarisation Anti-Globalisation & Warfare', Centre for Sustainable Urban and Regional Futures, Manchester, November 2002.

In an interview I conducted with Aviv Kokhavi, commander of the Paratrooper Brigade, he explained the principle that guided the battle.[6] What was interesting for me in his explanation of the principle of the battle was not so much the description of the action itself as the way he conceived its articulation.

6. In order to put this interview in context it is important to note that Kokhavi took time off from active service, like many career officers, to earn a university degree. He originally intended to study architecture, but ultimately pursued philosophy at the Hebrew University. In one of his many recent interviews in the press he claimed that his military practice is influenced to a great extent by both disciplines. Chen Kotes-Bar, 'Starring Him [Bekikhuvo],' in Ma'ariv, 22 April 2005 [Hebrew].

'This space that you look at, this room that you look at, is nothing but your interpretation of it. Now, you can stretch the boundaries of your interpretation, but not in an unlimited fashion, after all it must be bound by physics, as it contains buildings and alleys. The question is: How do you interpret the alley? Do you interpret it as a place, like every architect and every town planner, to walk through, or do you interpret it as a place that is forbidden to walk through? This depends only on interpretation. We interpreted the alley as a place forbidden to walk through, and the door as a place forbidden to pass through, and the window as a place forbidden to look through, because a weapon awaits us in the alley, and a booby trap awaits us behind the doors. This is because the enemy interprets space in a traditional, classical manner, and I do not want to obey this interpretation and fall into his traps. Not only do I not want to fall into his traps, I want to surprise him! This is the essence of war. I need to win. I need to emerge from an unexpected place. And this is what we tried to do.

This is why we opted for the methodology of moving through walls . . . Like a worm that eats its way forward, emerging at points and then disappearing. . . . I said to my troops, "Friends! This is not a matter of your choice! There is no other way of moving! If until now you were used to moving along roads and sidewalks, forget it! From now on we all walk through walls!"'

For anyone who might imagine that moving through walls is a relatively 'gentle' form of warfare, the following is a description of the sequence of the events: Soldiers assemble behind a wall. Using explosives or a large hammer, they break a hole large enough to pass through. Their charge through the wall is sometimes preceded by stun grenades or a few random shots into what is most often a private living room occupied by unsuspecting civilians. When the soldiers have passed through the party wall, the occupants are assembled and locked inside one of the rooms, where they are made to remain – sometimes for several days – until the operation is concluded, often without water, toilet, food or medicine. The unexpected penetration of war into the private domain of the home has been experienced by civilians in Palestine, just like in Iraq, as the most profound form of trauma and humiliation. A Palestinian woman identified as Aisha, interviewed by a journalist for the *Palestine Monitor*, Sune Segal, in November 2002, described the experience:

'Imagine it – you're sitting in your living room, which you know so well; this is the room where the family watches television together after the evening meal. . . . And, suddenly, that wall disappears with a deafening roar, the room fills with dust and debris, and through the wall pours one soldier after the other, screaming orders. You have no idea if they're after you, if they've come to take over your home, or if your house just lies on their route to somewhere else. The children are screaming, panicking. . . . Is it possible to even begin to imagine the horror experienced by a five-year-old child as four, six, eight, twelve soldiers, their faces painted black, submachine guns pointed everywhere, antennas protruding from their back-packs, making them look like giant alien bugs, blast their way through that wall?'[7]

7. Sune Segal, 'What Lies Beneath: Excerpts from an Invasion', in *Palestine Monitor*, November 2002; www. palestinemonitor.org/eyewitness/Westbank/what_lies_ beneath_by_sune_segal.html (9 June 2005); see also Nurhan Abujidi, 'Forced to Forget: Cultural Identity & Collective Memory/Urbicide Reference'. Durham Work Shop 24-25 November 2005, Durham, England.

Pointing to another wall now covered by a bookcase she adds:

IDF forces attack the Nablus enclave. Illustration OTRI, 2002

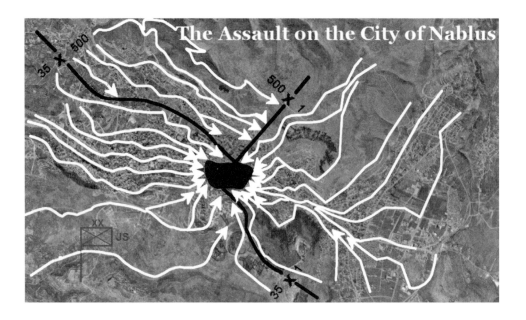

View over the Balata Refugee Camp adjacent to Nablus.
Photo Nir Kafri, 2003

Paratroopers moving through a ceiling in Nablus' old city centre. Photo OTRI (Operation Theory Research Institute), 2002

'And this is where they left. They blew up the wall and continued to our neighbour's house.'[8]

8. Segal, 'What Lies Beneath', op. cit. (note 8).

Shimon Naveh, a retired brigadier general, directs the Operational Theory Research Institute (closed May 2006), which is affiliated with the military and trains staff officers from the IDF and other militaries in 'operational theory' – defined in military jargon as somewhere between strategy and tactics. In an interview, Naveh summed up the mission of his institute, which was founded in 1996.

'We are like the Jesuit order. We attempt to teach and train soldiers to think. . . . We read Christopher Alexander (can you imagine?), we read John Forester, and other architects. We are reading Gregory Bateson, we are reading Clifford Geertz. Not myself, but our soldiers, our generals are reflecting on these kinds of materials. We have established a school and developed a curriculum that trains "operational architects".'[9]

9. Shimon Naveh, discussion following the talk, 'Dicta Clausewitz: Fractal Manoeuvre: A Brief History of Future Warfare in Urban Environments', delivered in conjunction with 'States Of Emergency: The Geography of Human Rights', a debate organized by myself and Anselm Franke as part of 'Territories Live', B'tzalel Gallery, Tel Aviv, 5 November 2004.

In a lecture, Naveh showed a diagram resembling a 'square of opposition' that plots a set of logical relationships between certain propositions referring to military and guerrilla operations. The corners were labelled with phrases such as *Difference and Repetition – The Dialectics of Structuring and Structure*; *Formless Rival Entities*; *Fractal Manoeuvre*; *Velocity vs. Rhythms*; *the Wahhabi War Machine*; *Postmodern Anarchists*; *Nomadic Terrorists*, mainly referencing the work of Deleuze and Guattari.[10] In our interview, I asked Naveh why Deleuze and Guattari?'[11] He replied:

10. Naveh, 'Dicta Clausewitz', op. cit (note 10); cf. among others, Naveh's titles to those in Gilles Deleuze and Félix Guattari, *A Thousand Plateaus, Capitalism and Schizophrenia* (New York/London: Continuum: 2004); Gilles Deleuze, *Difference and Repetition* (New York: Columbia University Press, 1995).

11. Eyal Weizman telephone interview with Shimon Naveh on 14 October 2005.

'Several of the concepts in *A Thousand Plateaus* became instrumental for us . . . allowing us to explain contemporary situations in a way that we could not have otherwise explained them. It problematized our own paradigms. . . . Most important was the distinction they have pointed out between the concepts of "smooth" and "striated" space . . . [which accordingly reflect] the organizational concepts of the "war machine"[12] and the "state apparatus" . . . In the IDF we now often use the term "to smooth out space" when we want to refer to operation in a space as if it had no borders. We

12. War machines, according to Deleuze and Guattari, are polymorphous and diffuse organizations characterized by their capacity for metamorphosis. They are made up of small groups that split up or merge with one another depending on contingency and circumstances. Deleuze and Guattari were aware that the state may willingly transform itself into a war machine. Similarly, in their discussion of 'smooth space', it is implied that this conception may lead to state domination.

try to produce the operational space in such a manner that borders do not affect us. Palestinian areas could indeed be thought of as "striated", in the sense that they are enclosed by fences, walls, ditches, roads blocks and so on . . . We want to confront the "striated" space of traditional, old-fashioned military practice [the way most IDF units presently operate] with smoothness that allows for movement through space that crosses any borders and barriers. Rather than contain and organize our forces according to existing borders, we want to move through them.'[13]

13. See also Shimon Naveh, *Asymmetric Conflict: An Operational Reflection on Hegemonic Strategies* (Tel Aviv: The Eshed Group for Operational Knowledge, 2005), 9.

And when I asked him if moving through walls was part of it, he explained: 'In Nablus, the IDF understood urban fighting as a spatial problem . . . Travelling through walls is a simple mechanical solution that connects theory and practice. Traversing boundaries is the definition of the condition of "smoothness".'[14]

14. Eyal Weizman telephone interview with Shimon Naveh on 14 October 2005.

Furthermore, in similar terms to those employed by contemporary philosophy, the military conceives of some of its own 'practice' as forms of research. Naveh claimed that since very little 'intelligence' can be produced about guerrilla and terror groups before military operations actually take place (often it is hard if not impossible for the military to penetrate these organizations), one of the only ways to gain knowledge regarding its organizational logic is to attack it. The assumption is that attacking the enemy in an unpredictable manner, randomly prodding it, will induce it to surface, reveal itself and assume shape, and when its shape becomes visible, it could be further attacked with more precision. This mode of action is what philosopher Brian Massumi recently defined as *incitatory* operation: militaries consciously contributing to the actual emergence of the threat they are purportedly there to pre-empt. 'Since the threat is proliferating in any case, your best option is to help make it proliferate more. The most effective way to fight an unspecified threat is to actively contribute to producing it . . . [causing] the enemy to emerge from its state of potential and take actual shape . . .'[15] In an interview I conducted with him, Naveh has put it these terms (no less): 'tacti-

15. Brian Massumi, 'Potential Politics and the Primacy of Preemption', *Theory & Event*, no. 2, vol. 10 (2007).

cal activity provides tools of inquiry for operational architects . . .' These actions lead thus to an inversion of the traditional relation of 'intelligence' to 'operation', or (in the terms of theory) 'research' to 'practice'. Naveh: 'Raids are a tools of research . . . they provoke the enemy to reveal its organization . . . Most relevant intelligence is not gathered as the basis upon which attacks are conducted, but attacks

Simon Naveh's PowerPoint slide marking 'connections' between theoretical categories that inform his operational theory. Note most categories refer to the work of Deleuze and Guattari.

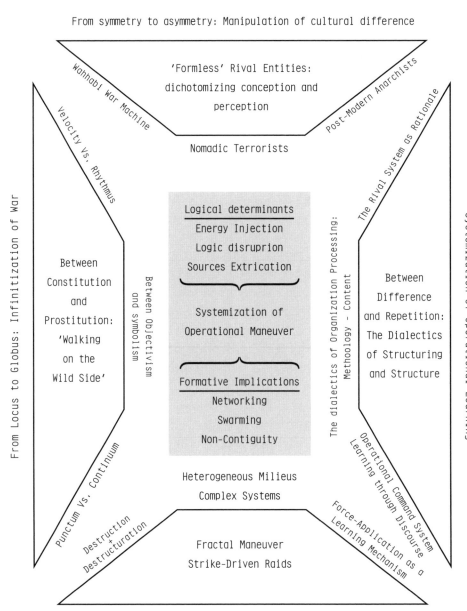

Manoeuvring through walls in the old city of Nablus.
Photo OTRI, 2005

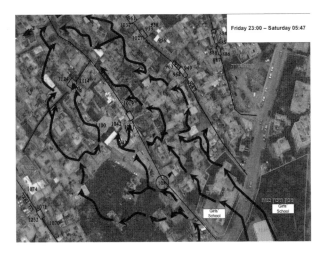

IDF and Palestinian manoeuvres through the old city centre
of Nablus, from a PowerPoint slide in Naveh's Tel Aviv
presentation. IDF did not move as expected through the main
roads, marked in solid black, but through the built fabric
itself. Dotted lines denote movement through buildings.

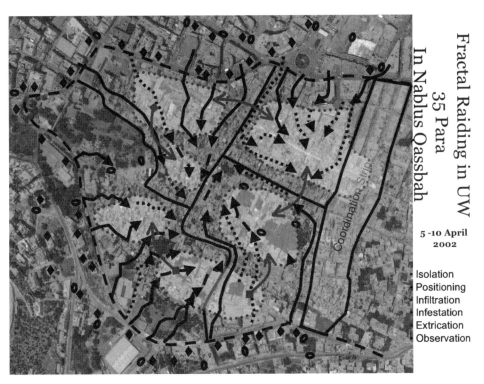

become themselves modes of producing knowledge about the enemy's system.' Within this mode of operation, practice supports research and not the other way around. Naveh further mentioned: 'Operative and tactical commanders depend on one another and learn the problems through constructing the battle narrative; action becomes knowledge, and knowledge becomes action. Without a decisive result possible, the main benefit of military operation is the very improvement of the [military] system as a system.'

To understand the IDF's tactics for moving through Palestinian urban spaces, it is necessary to understand how they interpret the by now familiar principle of 'swarming' – a term that has been a buzz word in military theory since the start of the Revolution in Military Affairs (RMA) in the 1980s (and the demonstration in 1991 during the Gulf War). The swarm manoeuvre was in fact adapted, at least in word, from the Artificial Intelligence principle of 'swarm intelligence', which assumes that problem-solving capacities are found in the interaction and communication of relatively unsophisticated agents (ants, birds, bees, soldiers) without (or with minimal) centralized control. 'Swarm intelligence' thus refers to the overall, combined intelligence of a system, rather than to the intelligence of its component parts. It is the system itself that learns through interaction and adaptation to emergent situations.[16]

16. Eric Bonabeau, Marco Dorigo and Guy Theraulaz, *Swarm Intelligence: From Natural to Artificial Systems* (Oxford: Oxford University Press, 1999); Sean J.A. Edwards, *Swarming on the Battlefield: Past, Present and Future* (Santa Monica: RAND, 2000); John Arquilla and David Ronfeldt (eds.), *Networks and Netwars: The Future of Terror, Crime, and Militancy* (Santa Monica: RAND, 2001).

The swarm exemplifies the principle of 'non-linearity' apparent in spatial, organizational, and temporal terms. The traditional manoeuvre paradigm, characterized by the simplified geometry of Euclidean order, is transformed, according to the military, into a complex 'fractal'-like geometry. Instead of fixed linear or vertical chains of command and communications, swarms are coordinated as polycentric networks with a horizontal form of communication, in which each 'autarkic unit' can communicate with the others without going through central command. The narrative of the battle plan is to be replaced by what the military calls 'the toolbox' approach,[17] according to which units receive the tools they need to deal with several given situations and scenarios, but cannot predict the order in which these events would actually occur. This non-linearity that is

17. Michel Foucault's description of theory as a 'toolbox' was originally developed in conjunction with Deleuze in a 1972 discussion; see Gilles Deleuze and Michel Foucault, 'Intellectuals and Power', in: Michel Foucault, *Language, Counter-Memory, Practice: Selected Essays and Interviews*, edited and introduction by Donald F. Bouchard (Ithaca: Cornell University Press, 1980), 206.

thus positioned at the very end of a very linear geometrical order, as well as a command system that is explained as 'non-hierarchical,' but is in fact located at the very tactical end of an inherently *hierarchical* system.

This may explain the fascination of the military with the spatial and organizational models and modes of operation advanced by theorists like Deleuze and Guattari.

Indeed, as far as the military is concerned, urban warfare is the ultimate postmodern form of warfare. Belief in a logically structured and single-track battle plan is lost in the face of the complexity and ambiguity of urban reality. 'It becomes,' as the same soldier later indicated, 'impossible to draw up battle scenarios or single-track plans to pursue.' Civilians become combatants, and combatants become civilians again. Identity can be changed as quickly as gender can be feigned: the transformation of women into fighting men can occur at the speed that it takes an undercover 'Arabized' Israeli soldier or a camouflaged Palestinian fighter to pull a machine gun out from under a dress. For a Palestinian fighter caught in the crosshairs of this battle, Israelis seem 'to be everywhere: behind, on the sides, on the right and on the left. How can you fight that way?'[18] Since Palestinian guerrilla fighters were sometimes manoeuvring in a similar manner, through pre-planned openings, most fighting took place in private homes. Some buildings became like layer cakes, with Israeli soldiers both above and below a floor where Palestinians were trapped.

18. Quoted in Yagil Henkin, 'The Best Way Into Baghdad', *The New York Times*, 3 April 2003, Op-Ed section, www.nytimes.com.

Critical theory has become crucial in Naveh's teaching and training. He explained during our interview: 'We employ critical theory primarily in order to critique the military institution itself – its fixed and heavy conceptual foundations. . . . Theory is important to us in order to articulate the gap between the existing paradigm and where we want to go. . . . Without theory, we could not make sense of different events that happen around us and that would otherwise seem disconnected. . . . We set up the Institute because we believed in education and needed an academy to develop ideas. . . . At present, the Institute has a tremendous impact on the military . . . [it has] become a subversive node within it. By training several high-ranking officers we filled the system [IDF] with subversive agents . . . who ask questions. . . . Some of the top brass are not embarrassed to talk about Deleuze or Tschumi.'[19]

19. Eyal Weizman telephone interview with Shimon Naveh on 14 October 2005.

Israeli engineers in the Tul Qarem Refugee Camp.
Photo Nir Kafri, 2001

My question to him was, why Tschumi?! 'The idea of disjunction embodied in Tschumi's book *Architecture and Disjunction* became relevant for us. . . . Tschumi had another approach to epistemology; he wanted to break with single-perspective knowledge and centralized thinking. He saw the world through a variety of different social practices, from a constantly shifting point of view. . . . [Tschumi] created a new grammar; he formed the ideas that compose our thinking.'[20]

20. Naveh is currently working on the Hebrew translation of Bernard Tschumi's *Architecture and Disjunction* (Cambridge, MA: MIT Press, 1997).

Again, the question, so why not Derrida and Deconstruction? 'Our generals are architects. . . . Tschumi conceptualized the relation between action, space and its representation. His *Manhattan Transcripts* gave us the tools to draw operational plans in a manner other than drawing simple lines on maps. Tschumi provided useful strategies for planning an operation. Derrida may be a little too opaque for our crowd. We share more with architects; we combine theory and practice. We can read, but we know as well how to build and destroy, and sometimes kill.'[21]

21. Eyal Weizman telephone interview with Shimon Naveh on 14 October 2005.

In addition to these theoretical positions, Naveh references such canonical elements of urban theory as the situationist practices of *dérive* (a method of drifting through a city based on what they referred to as *psychogeography*) and *détournement* (the adaptation of abandoned buildings for purposes other than those they were designed to perform). These ideas were of course conceived by Guy Debord and other members of the Situationist International as part of a general strategy to challenge the built hierarchy of the capitalist city and break down distinctions between private and public, inside and outside,[22] use and function, replacing private space with a 'borderless' public surface. References to the work of Georges Bataille, either directly or as cited in the writings of Tschumi, also speak of a desire to attack architecture. Bataille's own call to arms was meant to dismantle the rigid rationalism of a post-war order, to escape 'the architectural straitjacket', and to liberate repressed human desires.

22. A Palestinian Woman described her experience of the battle in this way: 'Go inside, he ordered in hysterical broken English. Inside! I am already inside! It took me a few seconds to understand that this young soldier was redefining inside to mean anything that is not visible, to him at least. My being 'outside' within the 'inside' was bothering him. Not only is he imposing a curfew on me, he is also redefining what is outside and what is inside within my own private sphere.' Segal, 'What Lies Beneath', op. cit. (note 8).

For Bataille, Tschumi and the situationists, the repressive power of the city is subverted by new strategies for moving through and across it. In the post-war period, when the broadly leftist theoretical ideas I have mentioned here were emerging, there was little confidence in the capacity of sovereign state structures to protect or further democracy. The 'micro-politics' of the time represented in many ways an attempt to constitute a mental and affective guerrilla fighter at the intimate levels of the body, sexuality and inter-subjectivity, an individual in whom the personal became subversively political. And as such, these micro-politics offered a strategy for withdrawing from the formal state apparatus into the private domain, which was later to extend outwards. While such theories were conceived in order to transgress the established 'bourgeois order' of the city, with the architectural element of the wall projected as solid and fixed, an embodiment of social and political repression. In the hands of the IDF, tactics inspired by these thinkers are projected as the basis for an attack on an 'enemy' city.

In no uncertain terms, education in the humanities – often believed to be the most powerful weapon *against* imperialism – is being appropriated as a powerful weapon *of* imperialism.

Although representing a spectrum of different positions, methods and periods, for Matta-Clark, Bataille, the situationists and Tschumi it was the repressive power of the capitalist city that should have been subverted. In the hands of the Israeli military, however, tactics inspired by these thinkers were projected as the basis for an attack on the little protected habitat of poor Palestinian refugees under siege.

In this context the transgression of domestic boundaries must be understood as the very manifestation of state repression. Hannah Arendt's understanding of the political domain of the classic city would agree with the equation of walls with law-and-order. According to Arendt, the political realm is guaranteed by two kinds of walls (or wall-like laws): the wall surrounding the city, which defined the zone of the political; and the walls separating private space from the public domain, ensuring the autonomy of the domestic realm.[23] The almost palindromic linguistic structure of law/wall helps to

23. Hannah Arendt, *The Human Condition* (Chicago: University of Chicago Press, 1998), 63-64.

further bind these two structures in an interdependency that equates built and legal fabric. The un-walling of the wall invariably becomes the undoing of the law. The military practice of 'walking through walls' – on the scale of the house or the city – links the physical properties of construction with this syntax of architectural, social and political orders. New technologies developed to allow soldiers to see living organisms through walls, and to facilitate their ability to walk and fire weapons through them, address thus not only the materiality of the wall, but also its very concept. With the wall no longer physi-

The process of walking through walls.
Video stills © Eyal Weizman

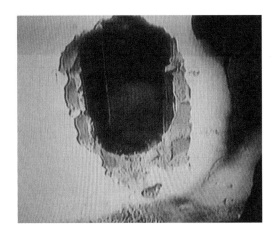 

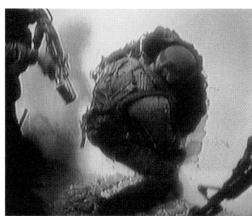
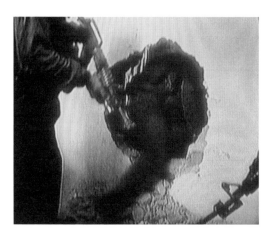

cally or conceptually solid or legally impenetrable, the functional spatial syntax that it created collapses. In 'the camp', Agamben's well-known observation follows the trace left by Arendt, 'city and house became indistinguishable'.[24] The breaching of the physical, visual and conceptual border/wall exposes new domains to political power, and thus draws the clearest physical diagram to the concept of the 'state of exception'.

24. Giorgio Agamben, *Homo Sacer: Sovereign Power and Bare Life* (Stanford: Stanford University Press, 1998), 187.

Future military operations in urban terrain will increasingly be dedicated to the use of technologies developed for the purpose of the 'un-walling of the wall'.[25] This is the architect's response to the logic of 'smart weapons'. The latter have paradoxically resulted in higher numbers of civilian casualties

25. Brian Hatton, 'The Problem of Our Walls', *The Journal of Architecture* 4 (Spring 1999), 71; Krzysztof Wodiczko, *Public Address* (Minneapolis: Walker Art Center, 1991).

simply because the illusion of precision gives the military-political complex the necessary justification to use explosives in civilian environments where they cannot be used without endangering, injuring or killing civilians.

The imagined benefits of 'smart destruction' and attempts to perform 'sophisticated' swarming thus bring more destruction over the long term than 'traditional' strategies ever did, because these ever-more deadly methods combined with the highly manipulative and euphoric theoretical rhetoric used to promulgate them have induced decision-makers to authorize their frequent use. Here another use of 'theory' as the ultimate 'smart weapon' becomes apparent. The military's seductive use of theoretical and technological discourse seeks to portray war as remote, sterile, easy, quick, intellectual, exciting and even economic (from their own point of view). Violence can thus be projected as tolerable, and the public encouraged to support it.

The interviews were conducted in August and September 2004 in both Hebrew (Kokhavi and Naveh) and English (Naveh), and documented on video by Nadav Harel and Zohar Kaniel. Translations from Hebrew are by the author.

A full version of this text appeared in 2006 on: http://roundtable.klein.org/files/roundtable/weizman_lethal%20theory.pdf

John Armitage

In the Cities of the Beyond

An Interview with Paul Virilio

At the request of *Open*, the cultural theoretician John Armitage interviewed the French urbanist and philosopher Paul Virilio (b. 1932, Paris). A discussion on the future of the city.

Virilio's futuristic writings on war zones, architecture and critical theory have appeared in many books, journals, and exhibition catalogs. An enduring theme has been the question of critical space, a question addressed in both his 1975 *Bunker Archeology* exhibition at the Musée des Arts Décoratifs and his 2009 'Native Land: Stop Eject' joint exhibition with Raymond Depardon at the Fondation Cartier pour l'Art Contemporain. Now inspiring countless interdisciplinary researchers in the arts, the humanities, and the social sciences, Virilio's investigations into the impact of new information and communications technologies, into the effects of mobile phones, video cameras, and the Internet, are above all concerned with their reconfiguration of cities such as Amsterdam. Theoretically sophisticated yet accessible to anybody interested in the relationship between the arts and inner-city anxieties, the geopolitics of public space, speed, and the contemporary technological revolution, Virilio's interview with John Armitage is part of a captivating discussion that concentrates on Virilio's *The University of Disaster* (2007) and *Le Futurisme de l'instant: Stop-Eject* (2009).[1]

1. See Paul Virilio, *L'Université du désastre* (Paris: Editions Galilée, 2007) and Paul Virilio *Le Futurisme de l'instant : Stop-Eject* (Paris: Editions Galilée, 2009).

JOHN ARMITAGE Professor Virilio, before we talk about your conceptualization of contemporary cities, can we explore the place of war as the main driving force behind your theoretical attempts to further our knowledge of technology and the city?

PAUL VIRILIO First of all, I am a war child. But I am also a child of the city. Furthermore, the Second World War, which was the war of my youth, was not only an urban war but also a hyper-technical war; a war involving the means of transportation, armoured vehicles, the aerial bombardment of cities, the development and use of telecommunications, radio, radar, and so on. Thus I am a child of a war where technology was the central element in the destruction of cities. This last is very important because, as we know, cities have been, from the outset, sites of technology. Technology was not primarily born in the fields or in the mountains. Technology was for the most part born in cities, through the development of arts and crafts and through the work of artists and artisans. By the time of the Second World War, of course, technology and modern industry were concentrated in modern cities and in their suburbs. As a result, during the Second World War, it was, above all, modern cities that had to be destroyed.

JA How does your stance as a critic of the art of technology add to our appreciation of war, technology and cities?

PV Let me explain: just as one might say 'I am a critic of painting', of the visual arts, of sculpture, or even of architecture, one can also say that 'I am a critic of the art of technology'.[2] Yet my position or response to your question is really that the study and explanation of war, technology and cities are, for me at least, all bound up together.

2. Virilio was presented with France's 'National Award for Criticism' for his entire oeuvre in 1987.

> JA Perhaps, in that case, we can begin to address the central themes associated with your conception of cities? What, for example, is the relationship between cities and the state for you, between cities and political power? As far as I understand it, for you, the 'real time' of information and communications technologies, of the Internet, mobile phones, and so forth, now overshadows the real space of cities. But what do such developments mean for the destiny of what might be called geographically based or geopolitical cities or for the fate of what the urban sociologist Saskia Sassen labels in her book *The Global City*?

PV For me, cities are first and foremost places or locations. However, I want to stress that, in the West at least, cities are also places or markers of the state. Cities were in the first place *city-states*. It was only after the stage of city-states that they became part of nation-states and, today, of federations of nation-states such as the European Union. Cities are therefore places where the accumulation of power takes place. Urban agglomerations are sites of accumulation, not simply of wealth, but also of power. Accordingly, cities can be conceived of as states-within-the-state, as the original state of today's nation-states. Before developing into the 'megapolis', into the 'megalopolis', cities functioned in line with the logic of the geopolitics of city-states and nation-states.

Nowadays, though, I argue that we have arrived at a critical threshold regarding cities. This is because, very simply, today, as you remark, the real time of information and communications technologies surpasses the real space of cities. We are thus becoming aware, and I *insist* on this very important point, of the possibility that what you call geopolitical cities are now at an end. Indeed, geopolitical cities are giving way to what I call, in *Le Futurisme de l'instant*, 'cities of the beyond'. Leaving geopolitical cities behind, such cities of the beyond are 'meteo-political' cities or cities based on a sort of atmospheric politics related to the immediacy, ubiquity and instantaneity of information and communications technologies. Unlike geopolitical cites, the cities of the beyond are not anchored in urban concentration, in agglomeration, or even in accumulation but, rather, in the acceleration of the electromagnetic waves of information and communications technologies.

In complete contrast to Sassen's conception of London, New York and Tokyo as focal points within the networks of global finance capitalism, as supposed 'postmodern' 'global cities', I propose that the acceleration of cities brought about by information and communications technologies, the acceleration that is presently rushing headlong towards us, is not that of Sassen's global city but that of the *'city-world'*!

> JA Yet what is the importance of your own work on the acceleration of the cities of the beyond or what you call the city-world? What, for instance, are the main changes that are happening within the cities of the beyond, within these apparently technologized and instantaneous megalopolises of globalization?

PV The significance of the accelerated cities of the beyond is linked to the instantaneity, ubiquity and immediacy of information and communications technologies based on electromagnetic waves. For such electromagnetic waves are the key causal factors behind what I call, in *The University of Disaster*, 'photosensitive inertia', a new regime of visibility wherein the temporal perspective experiences a transmutation to such a degree that, today, time is exposed at the speed of electromagnetic waves. The temporal order thus becomes the order of absolute acceleration, an order of light, or what I call 'luminocentrism', where the three tenses – of past, present, and future – can no longer be described as a *chronology* but, rather, must be characterized as a *chronoscopy*.[3] Here, the real time of interactivity not only transports us to a kind of intangible 'place' but also becomes *the* new ethereal 'place' of the city. Crucially, this indefinable 'place' usurps all our previous understandings of the reality and materiality of geopolitical cities, of, if you like, particular real places and specific material cities. In other words, geography is replaced by what I term 'trajectography'. With photosensitive inertia and trajectography the inertial properties of objects are increasingly dismissed. What is advocated, instead, is our immersion in a photosensitive inertia, our submergence in a trajectory of endless acceleration, so much so that this trajectography has now reached the speed of light.

3. See Virilio, *L'Université du désastre*, op. cit. (note 2), chapter 3.

Similarly, identity is more and more substituted by what I call 'traceability'. What I mean by traceability is that, today, all our gesticulations, our slightest actions, are observed, sensed and highlighted by the techniques and technologies of computerized tracking. Each and every one of us is now under the controlling gaze of various detectors, of video cameras, of radars, and of other forms of control and detection, such as the electromagnetic waves carrying the messages of our appropriately named 'cell' phones. Abandoning the ancient trajectory of our former extended journeys, we have today arrived, almost unnoticeably, at a 'place' where 'on the spot' gesticulations, signals, motions and waves are now a vital sign of our growing photosensitive inertia, an inertia that will, tomorrow, root all of us to the spot.

Something is at work here that is truly extraordinary. To be sure, it is the idea that, henceforth, cities are, as the English architects of the Archigram group of the 1960s used to argue, 'instant cities'. Yet these movable cities, these technological cities of photosensitive inertia, are cities of insubstantial, almost atmospheric, 'places', cities where the structures of geopolitical cities are replaced by trajectories, by acceleration and by the gesticulations of traceability.

It is for these reasons and those that I stated before that I am against Sassen's idea of the global city. But this opposition is not simply because of my concern with automated vision technologies and the techniques of pursuit. It is also because, as has been demonstrated by Non-Governmental Organizations like Christian Aid as well as the United Nations, the coming megalopolises of 30 to 40 – or even 50 million plus inhabitants are the real future cities of the beyond. For when one says that the global city is our future that does not merely mean a future of detectors, of cameras and of radar sensors and mobile phones, but, in addition, a future in which the megalopolis has 'won', so to speak. We have to ask ourselves: are cities of 70 million inhabitants – I am thinking here of New Delhi in 50 years, as has already been forecast – a triumph for geopolitical cities or a failure of geopolitical cities? For me, the dawn of the megalopolises is the *absolute failure, the absolute end, of geopolitical cities as we have known them*. What is happening here is not simply the disappearance of geopolitical cities, and of geo-strategies, for that matter, but, besides, the appearance of instantaneous electromagnetic cities, of cities founded on waves, on photosensitive inertia, on immediacy and ubiquity. Thus *it is the world that has become the city*, an instant city of interactivity and photosensitive inertia, of elusive public 'places' that eliminate even the idea of the capital city itself. The supersession of real space by real-time information and communications technologies is therefore a break without precedent and one of the key transformative spatiotemporal shifts of the twenty-first century.

JA To what extent is the general take-over of real space by real-time information and communications technologies a result of the spatiotemporal break brought about by the particular supersession of the inertial telephone by the mobile telephone? How does the technology of the mobile telephone impact upon the space of the body and the temporality of subjectivity?

PV Let me explain: today, cities are not real places that we actually inhabit. Rather, in the era of real time, in the age of technologized screens that accompany our increasingly displaced lifestyles, cities are a series of corporeal and technological trajectories, made up not so much of 'televiewers' as what I term in *The University of Disaster* 'mobiviewers'.[4] In this respect, the course of our lives is no longer attached to our homes, even if we 'live in'   4. Ibid., chapter 5.
a large metropolis. This is because, as addicts of acceleration, we are becoming post-sedentary men and women who are now *at home everywhere*. Whether we are on a train or in an airplane, it no longer matters. This is because our 'place' of residence is, thanks to the mobile phone revolution, *everywhere*. Yet, like nomads, we are *at home both everywhere and nowhere*, and, I would suggest, seemingly permanently veering off track.

Consider ordinary pedestrians. Are they not in a condition that is close to being intoxicated? In reality, they have become what can only be described as accidental choreographers, much like handicapped people. Without any kind of field of vision relating to the objects and other pedestrians along the street, such people concentrate instead on the spatiotemporal realm of the audiovisible, on the people they are talking to on their mobile phones. In short, pedestrians no longer see anything in front of themselves. The question is: What do these mobile phone practices tell us about contemporary cities? Surely, they tell us at the very least that we are now faced with a new spatiality of the body, with a new 'body technology'. This body technology, moreover, seems to involve people rejoicing in a new kind of corporeal or postural drift. The rambling actions and lopsided appearance of contemporary pedestrians is therefore a good example of how they are now unfamiliar even with the immediate vicinity around which they walk. Such lonely individuals desert the immediacy of their surroundings because they are totally absorbed in the collective fantasy of a far-away audiovisible figure that will, so they believe, fulfil their desires to the detriment of any genuine human encounter.

These solitary individuals are what I call in *The University of Disaster* 'object-oriented' but, critically, '*subject-*   5. Ibid.
disoriented'.[5] For them, cities are not 'places' they inhabit; their 'home' is no longer in the geopolitical cities. As alternatives, the cities they 'inhabit' or, rather, which actually *inhabit them*, are cities which are *on*

them and, with radio waves everywhere, *in* them as well. For, unlike in the nineteenth or twentieth century, we no longer live *within* cities because cities live *within us*. At this point, and although we could focus once more on the idea of acceleration and the technological revolutions of transportation and transmission associated with the nineteenth or twentieth century, it is equally important, nevertheless, to insist that cities are no longer 'ours', that is, they are no longer 'our places', in the sense of being 'our home'. There are without doubt a number of precedents for this sort of urban dislocation. Our sense of being 'at home' was, as we know, eventually penetrated by the telephone, by the radio, television, etcetera, throughout the twentieth century. But today we are already at the stage where cities, as entities that are *on* us, as things that we literally *take with us*, are making the metropolis almost uninhabitable as people attempt to move around on a daily basis with the entire city strapped to their bodies. With the mobile phone revolution, then, cities are now *us*. And cities have become something like a snail shell on our bodies. These, therefore, are not merely cities of the beyond but also, I might add, cities of *transplantations*. Meanwhile, other people have become nothing more than impediments to us or our opponents.

And so, our long appreciated freedom of movement, the first freedom of all living beings, is giving way to a kind of incarceration within a photosensitive inertia, an incarceration not within a room or within the geopolitical cities of the twentieth century, but within the cities of the beyond, the twenty-first-century cities of electromagnetic waves.

JA Is there a connection between losing our freedom of movement, between becoming imprisoned within a photosensitive inertia, and contemporary forms of economic accumulation within the cities of the beyond?

PV Many economic analysts of large cities are still trapped within investigations that foreground the logic of metropolitan economic accumulation. They are still ensnared within the realm of the quantitative. In contrast, I believe that we have entered the age of acceleration. As a matter of fact, acceleration has now superseded economic accumulation. Acceleration is, for example, one of the key causes of the current global economic crisis. Actually, the present global crisis of capital *is* the crisis of accumulation as such. I remind you that capital is not just accumulation but also acceleration. The first bankers, for instance, were horsemen. Bankers were knights before becoming ship owners and seafarers. So, initially at least, in historical terms, accumulation prevailed over acceleration. Of course, the acceleration of a horse or a ship is laughable when compared to the power of accumulation we have witnessed throughout history in cities such as Venice, London, and Amsterdam. But today *it is the reverse*! Economic accumulation has been superseded by acceleration! This is because the speed of light, the instantaneity, ubiquity, and the immediacy of electromagnetic waves all accelerate accumulation. The current global economic crisis is thus not only an economic crisis but also a crisis of accumulation brought about by the overthrow of capital by ceaseless acceleration.

> JA Nevertheless, what are the consequences for the city and its inhabitants of the existing global economic crisis of accumulation detonated by the domination of capital by unending acceleration?

PV As I have said many times before, both the city and the earth are too small to accommodate the propaganda and consequences of so-called twentieth century progress, especially as our urban and ecological footprint grows ever larger and deeper. We must recognize that, as city dwellers, we have entered a period where we are dealing with the *consequences* of twentieth century progress. Technoscience, geography, economics and politics are all confronted with their own limits, with the restrictions not purely of a now completed globalization but also with the limits of the planet itself that, today, reveals all too clearly its, and our own, troubled history. This period of consequences is an incontrovertible fact and is the product of the damage wrought by the propaganda of twentieth-century progress.

However, such a realization does not necessarily lead me directly from the current global economic crisis of accumulation to a call for the creation of a new kind of political ecology. Obviously, political ecology is important. But so too is the development of a political economy of speed, especially given that political economy in the twenty-first century is not simply about the accumulation of wealth but also about acceleration. Acceleration, therefore, must be placed at the forefront of our concerns because it is now at the heart of the accumulation of wealth in the cities, of the accumulation of knowledge, and the very reality of all our social lives that are increasingly driven by unrelenting interactivity. Today, we are facing a major historical phenomenon that, for example, Marxism never anticipated: that a political economy of acceleration has come to supersede the political economy of accumulation. Thus what is very important right now is the construction of a political economy of speed.

JA I can appreciate how economic accumulation is related to acceleration and to the need for a political economy of speed. But how is acceleration linked to geographical agglomeration, to cities that are, for all intents and purposes, spatially immobile?

PV Acceleration and geographical agglomeration are connected, particularly in relation to cities, and have been associated, since at least the time of ancient Rome. The ancient Romans' simplest symbol of the city of Rome, for instance, traced out a circle with a cross through it. Indeed, this symbol was also the symbol of ancient Roman city planning, and was used together with the term *decumanus cardo* or east-west and north-south oriented roads. But what is important here is not only that the city was, even in Roman times, divided into allotments and buildings, but also that what prevails is the tracing out, the marks, or the charting or mapping not so much of stoppage or of stasis but of *movement*.

Consequently, even at the point where the Romans, or anyone else either before or since for that matter, decided to allot or build a parliament building here, or an entertainment complex there, they were, in effect, tracing out movement. *The city is movement!* One cannot build a city without first of all tracing, marking, charting, mapping out, or drawing lines of movement! Evidently, life in the ancient world of the Roman city was not *motorized* as cities are today. In that sense, Roman cities were far from being based on technology in the way that cities are nowadays. Nonetheless, they were cities founded on movement. This is hardly surprising since all ancient societies were 'animated' societies, societies of movement, and movement of the most physical kind possible given that they were rooted in the soldier on horseback. Yet, as I indicated before, the socially dominant factor has always been acceleration. It has always been the *speed* of the soldier on horseback that mattered most. Clearly, these days, people are much more concerned with the speed of their urban telecommunications connections and transmissions. But the chief problems, ever since the birth of cities, have always been those associated with the tracing, with the marking, and charting or mapping of movement, with animation, motorization and, today, telecommunication. So, although I suggested earlier that I am currently researching the contemporary question of traceability, the fact is that the problem of tracing, of traceability, is not new at all. Rather, traceability has been a problem that has overshadowed the question of the city from the beginning. Questions concerning the city and movement, then, have always taken precedence over questions concerning the city and inertia. It is equally important to remember that ancient societies were *nomadic* societies, societies predicated on movement. Human sedentary life is thus but a secondary phenomenon, a mere moment in the longer human history of a life lived in movement.

> JA As a final point, and even though our discussion of ancient Roman cities, of stoppages, stasis, nomadism and movement have been extremely productive, I would like to ask: What is happening to sedentary life in contemporary cities? What are the key terms here? Stoppage? Stasis? Nomadism? Is the present moment one of human stasis or one of human movement?

PV As I have already indicated, unlike ancient Roman cities, or even nineteenth- and twentieth-century cities, the cities of the beyond are not derived from stoppages and stasis but from the *explosion* of former geographical agglomerations, from the *break-up* of geopolitical cities, and from the contemporary *exodus* from the materiality of existing cities. The cities we are headed for are cities of immateriality, of telecommunications, air corridors and high-speed railway lines, of airports, railway stations and harbours *as* cities. That is why in *Le Futurisme de l'instant* I write not of urbanism or suburbanism but of an accelerated '*exurbanism*', which is, by means of a range of technologies, such as the Internet, gearing up to displace the urbanism and the suburbanism of the cities of the industrialized era.[6] Exurbanism is nothing like the sedentary urbanism of the recent past because contemporary societies and cities are increasingly *nomadic*. The cities of the beyond are cities of movement, cities of migrants, of temporary shelter, and of segregation by the newly resurgent city-state. These are cities of '*foreigners*' living in steel containers in Rotterdam, Amsterdam and in other places. And, as urbanism and suburbanism yield to the critical space that is '*exurbia*', to urban *up-rootedness*, what follows is the outsourcing and subsequent flight of important economic enterprises. Essential businesses, inclusive of their research and development laboratories and other facilities – the most valuable part of any economic enterprise today – are then leaving their traditionally localized spaces of production. Such industries and companies are thus heading for the externalized 'centre' of the cities of the beyond, for those 'cities' no longer based on sedentary urbanism but based on a nomadism or an accelerated urban exodus wherein *no one feels at home anywhere*. Remember what I said to you about tracing, marking, charting, mapping and the allotment of buildings in space and time. *These are not mere words!* In truth, we are currently tracing and

6. See Virilio *Le Futurisme de l'instant*, op. cit. (note 2), chapter 1.

planning cities of the beyond with an eye to finally leaving the twentieth-century city behind. We are seeking to achieve an exurbanism that entails both the end of sedentary urbanism and also *the 'resettlement' of the entire world*! This sort of development amounts to nothing less than the end of geopolitical cities, the end of the rural-urban exodus, at least in the advanced countries, and the beginning of the cities of the beyond.

In other words, we are 'exiting' towards cities that are founded on movement. Also, as I have always argued, even in the geopolitical cities, in the cities where belonging, centres and peripheries obtained, the 'exit' – of the railway station, of the seaport, of the airport – has always been extremely significant. Certainly, this is why the subtitle of *Le Futurisme de l'instant* is *Stop-Eject*![7]   7. Ibid.
For what we are faced with here is a movement of both stoppage *and* ejection, of 'places' and cities *of* ejection. *Stop-Eject* therefore refers to events of monumental proportions, of unheard of population growth, for example, of instantaneous transmission and high-speed travel that is currently resulting in billions of people becoming dislocated in the twenty-first century. Yet, at the same time, and as inhabitants of the city-world, we are also being told to leave it, to 'get out', and to become exiles or outcasts from the world of both physical and human geography.

However, the essential point, as I have been stressing throughout this interview, is the domination of the real time of global information and communications technologies over the real space of Sassen's supposed global city. Speed, for instance, not only signals a form of power, a form of political economy, but also the end of geography. The instantaneity of contemporary speed for that reason brings with it a kind of 'spatial pollution'. This is what I have called elsewhere the 'old age of the world' because, like human beings, as the world grows old, time seems to pass ever more rapidly. But, today, we can also see that accelerated transportations and telecommunications force the world to operate under instantaneous conditions that nevertheless *have a real impact* on geography, history and on our sense of real time and real space. But much more than the end of geography is at stake as the pollution of distances and substances takes hold. For the instantaneity of acceleration also signals the end of history, not in the sense that Francis Fukuyama argued, but in the sense that we have come to the end of the natural historical and spatial scale of earthly things, such as a human-centred sense of distance. As the former enormity of the world is reduced to nothing more than *speed-space*, then, geopolitics, geo-strategy, the human spatial scale of the city and the nation-state are accordingly obliterated in favour of the realm of the urban *instant*, a realm that is not simply far removed from the physical geography of the real world, but that is also the province of technologized trace-ability and contemporary trajectography, of, in other words, an almost uninhabitable planet.

'In the Cities of the Beyond' was conducted by John Armitage at 'L'Argoat Bar and Restaurant', La Rochelle, France, on 22 May 2009. This interview would not have occurred without the sustained curiosity, friendship and largesse of Paul Virilio, Patrice Riemens and, needless to say, Diiinooos! I would like to convey my heartfelt gratitude to them all.

Transcription and translation from French into English: Patrice Riemens.

column

TOM MCCARTHY

MEXICO CITY, AMSTERDAM

In the mid 1990s I lived in Amsterdam. My accommodation, then, was a well-appointed squat. My downstairs neighbour was a Serbian performance artist whose work consisted of dragging his hands down windowpanes. Perhaps not entirely coincidentally, one of my flat's windows was missing a sheet of glass. After measuring the hole and trudging off to have a new sheet cut, I boarded a tram whose driver refused to transport me, instructing me, in Dutch, to disembark. I didn't understand, of course; a fellow passenger translated for me, adding, in a reasoned, explanatory tone, that 'if the tram crashed, shards of glass might hurt us'. The emphasis and inflection of his words made it crystal clear that *us* meant the Dutch passengers, not me.

As the tram pulled off again and I stood on the pavement watching it recede, I pictured the only tram crash I'd ever heard of: the one in Mexico City in 1925 in which the artist Frieda Kahlo, seated behind an artisan transporting a small bag of gold dust, found herself both skewered by a metal pole and gilted by the ruptured package. The event formed the basis of her work, which repeatedly shows her transfigured, by some glorious catastrophe, into a tortured icon.

The violent, Catholic splendour of Kahlo's Mexico seemed very far away that day from safety-conscious, Puritan Holland. And yet the Dutch have been living in the shadow of catastrophe since their country's inception. The very land on which they build their houses and through which they run their trams is stolen from a sea that wants it back, protected by dams and polders that defy the basic principle that you can't live lower than sea level. I imagine that Holland first enters the imagination of most of the World's non-Dutch children, as it did mine, via the fable of the little boy who, noticing a small hole in the sea wall, plugs it with his finger and stays there all night to save the town. His civic-mindedness is a Dutch feature, as an English carpenter, encountered in a bar, explained to me one evening soon after my ejection from the tram: 'In the old days, every citizen, irrespective of their wealth or status, had to put in two or three days every year at shoring up the sea wall. Their logic was that if the dyke goes, we're all fucked.'

I wondered who the *we* referred to this time. Puritan theology divides the world into an *us* and a *them*: within a predetermined universe that will end, soon, in apocalypse, a few have been selected – pre-selected – as Elect, the ones who will be saved; the others, indeed the vast majority, however, are the Preterite, or damned. The script's been written, and it can't be changed. But acting in a way consistent with being one of the Elect confers upon the actor an Elect status – one that, since it's not the actor but the writer (God) determining his actions, becomes its own proof, its own confirmation: a logic as self-contained as a polder.

The bar in which the carpenter explained the collective barrage-shoring custom to me lay on the Zeedijk, the location (as its name suggests) of Amsterdam's old sea dyke. The street is full of late-night bars. There used to be one there named *Mexico City*; Camus used it as the setting for *The Fall*. In the novel, 'judge-penitent' Jean-Baptiste Clamence talks, like my carpenter, to an anonymous narrator, comparing Amsterdam's layout, with its concentric canals, to the topography of Dante's *Inferno*. Nowadays, outside the Zeedijk's bars, on the street itself, foreign drug addicts shake and shuffle as they wait for their next hit. While their Dutch counterparts are provided with prescription heroin, these people, modern Preterite, are kept firmly beyond the polder of social inclusion, scraping its window-pane from the outside. For them, the apocalypse has come, and is repeating on an endless loop: each day is a long, slow catastrophe.

Camus's Clamence dates his own fall to his failure, some years ago, to act to save a woman from drowning: he, like her, has sunk, lower even than sea level. During the short time I lived in Amsterdam, my childhood image of the Dutch boy with his finger in the dam mutated, till it grew into a strangely English one: a boy pulling his finger from the hole, his face, no longer innocent, replaced with the malicious, leering one of Johnny Rotten, two maniacal white eyes glaring from its centre like marble chrysanthemums.

Artists' contribution by
Adi Kaplan and Shahar Carmel

Fugue

The artist duo Adi Kaplan (b. 1967)
and Shahar Carmel (b. 1958) have
worked and lived together in Tel
Aviv since 1993. Their paintings,
cartoons and performances offer
biting criticism of the social and
political reality in Israel. For
this issue, Kaplan and Shahar took
a trip to Amsterdam in the midst of
civil war in the year 2030. This
contribution is based on a short
story called *The Leader* by Avigdor
Hameiry (1951).

P.2

FOUND ALIVE IN THE WATER BY DEFICIENT MAN

"IT FELT AS IF TEN MINUTES

HAD PASSED BUT IT WAS ALMOST

THREE WEEKS"

THE MYSTERIOUS CASE OF THE MISSING TV ANCHOR

UNSOLVED CASE TV ANCHOR:

VICTIM OR TRAITOR

p.3

PLEASE BEHAVE NATURALLY

p.4   left:

PERMITS OFFICE

➤

CONTROL POST

NORTH

1000M

right:

CAUGHT BY

SURVEILLANCE CAMERA'S

THE RESCUED TV ANCHOR

VICTIM OR TRAITOR?

P.5

SUDDENLY FORGOT

HER IDENTITY

WHO WAS I THEN?

WHO AM I NOW?

DOCTOR SAYS

DISSOCIATIVE FUGUE

34 MISSING SINCE

p.6

A WHOLE SET OF INFORMATION ABOUT

ONE'S AUTOBIOGRAPHY

GOES OFF LINE

p.7

DEAR PASSENGER:

SCOUR UNDER YOUR SEAT FOR SUSPECTED OBJECTS!

REPORT IMMEDIATELY TO THE DRIVER!

REMEMBER! AWARENESS PREVENTS DISASTER!

I was the last among his former friends, who used to sleep with him before the leap in the nights beneath the bridges and beg for alms with him during the days. His stupidity loomed, grew greater from day to day, silenced his tongue, and he used to look out at the world like a calf. That was his name among us: the Calf.

One day he became sick. I took him to the clinic and they stuck a needle into his behind and told him to come back in a week. Afterwards he started having trouble swallowing, and broke out in a florid rash. Right away I knew he'd contracted the plague. I moved away from him in disgust and said: 'So what will you do now without me?' He looked at me out of his round, brown eyes.

After awhile I heard – and couldn't believe it – that the Calf was resurrected. He'd found work in a large media corporation. What he had to say was being listened to, taken into account. Finally I heard: a leader. That was beyond our simple comprehension. 'Such things are possible,' my friend the Colt said to me. 'It has happened before that somebody got a knock on the head and began to write poetry!'

I went to listen to his speech on television. It seemed to me that I was hearing the mooing of a calf, there's that kind of melody in his voice. Then I saw how everyone was listening to him and the blood went to my head. 'Hah! The Calf is mooing!' I said to one of my neighbors in the crowd. To that the fellow replied with barely restrained fury: 'Could be. That's why it's best you listen.'

And he turned immediately to his neighbors and said, 'This deficient is a terrorist!' Soldiers arrived, took me into detention, and after a week they threw me out of town. Since then, I've been dragging my deficient soul through the free zone and slipping into the city to make a living.

Yesterday as I was returning home, walking along the canal, I saw a woman floating in the water. Without thinking, I jumped in and pulled her out. She was alive. She turned out to be an important lady, because people came, and police and the media. I was questioned a lot, and it was only late at night that they left me alone. In the morning I was notified that the leader wants to talk to me. That's where I'm going *now*.

At the Institute for Human Research the Calf sat on a simple chair. I took a good look – it was really him. I sat down with a grimace of pain. My kidneys were troubling me because of being sprayed. He sat and said nothing. I was getting tired of it.

'Listen, Cat,' he finally said, 'are you still alive and sentient?' 'No thanks to you,' I said to him. 'And why not?' he asked with damned ease. 'Millions think they're alive thanks to me.' I laughed

in his face: 'I bet you think a million idiots are smarter than one! Idiot!' I got up and turned to go, but then the door opened and into the room came the media and the girl I'd rescued from the canal. The Calf rose from his chair. 'Come in, come in,' he said, spreading his hands. 'Come here, Cat,' he said to me. He put an arm over the girl's shoulders and struck the pose of a leader. I ignored them and continued walking.

The Calf ran after me. 'Wait, Cat, wait!' he cried, standing on the threshold of the door. 'One photo! That's all! I'll make it worth your while!' But I stepped outside, with his security guard following me, and everyone heard and saw the Calf yelling after me and asking me to stay. But that wasn't the end of it...

The girl I'd rescued came running. She caught my hand and said: 'Dissociative fugue. That's what I had. I just went jogging, you know, that's all, on my morning run, and the next thing I remember is riding in the ambulance. It felt as if only ten minutes had passed, but it was really three weeks.' I gently released her grip and continued walking. When I got out of the city and was walking along the canal, something very silly happened: I saw another one in the water.

Wietske Maas and Matteo Pasquinelli

The City Devouring Itself

Urbanibalism in Times of World Wars, Insurgent Communes and Biopolitical Sieges

In times of war, the accepted food chain is broken and the city becomes 'edible'. It starts to cannibalize itself, according to Wietske Maas and Matteo Pasquinelli, who use various historical examples to prove their point. With this 'urbanibalisme', as they call it, as their motive, they've developed a recipe for a therapeutic beverage, *Ferment Brussels*, to bring a toast to a communal lifestyle as the antidote to rising forms of nationalism.

'No work, no spuds. No work, no turnips, no tanks, no flying fortress. No victory.'

Propaganda film *Victory Garden* issued by the US Department of Agriculture, 1943

'Un espace de vie privé de Tiers paysage serait comme un esprit privé de l'inconscient. Cette situation parfaite, sans démon, n'existe dans aucune culture connue.'

Gilles Clément, *Manifeste du Tiers Paysage*, 2004

Dig for Victory! England at War and Spade, 1941-1945

Urban farming was a serious undertaking long before today's food crisis and the upsurge of sustainability jargon and art avant-*gardens*. City acreages have historically been cultivated in preparation for and in times of war. In the early Middle Ages, many towns were designed with plots inside the defence walls in order to grow a self-sufficient source of vegetables during recurrent sieges. Also the *hortus conclusus,* the cloister of the abbey, was an 'enclosure' of the countryside to be cultivated and protected from attacks by barbarians.[1] Today, in a Cuba still under US embargo, roof-tops, public squares and collapsed buildings are inventively turned into sites for growing everyday food.

1. Rob Aben and Saskia de Wit, *The Enclosed Garden: History and Development of the Hortus Conclusus and Its Reintroduction into the Present-Day Urban Landscape* (Rotterdam: 010 Publishers, 1999).

During the Second World War, as the Germans sank many of the vessels bringing food to Britain, the campaign *Dig for Victory!* surged to a national imperative. High-yield war gardens helped Brits save fuel and allocate more domestic money for the troops and military arms. US propaganda already stated clearly: 'A victory garden is like a share in an airplane factory. It helps win the war and pays dividends too.'[2] As Carloyn Steel points out: 'By the end of the war, an estimated 1.5 million allotments in Britain were providing a tenth of the nation's food, and one half of all its fruits and vegetables . . . It often takes the disruption of normal food supplies to reveal a city's productive potential.'[3]

2. Claude Wickard, Secretary of Agriculture, in *Victory Garden*, a film issued by the US Department of Agriculture, 1943 (*www.archive.org/details/victory_garden*).

3. Carolyn Steel, *Hungry City: How Food Shapes Our Lives* (London: Chatto & Windus, 2008), 316.

The scenario of war, more than a well-regulated city ecology, forces a recognition of the overlooked nature across the urban landscape. This space is what the gardener Gilles Clément refers to as the *third landscape*, a 'residue' full of biological potential that grows between the first landscape of nature and the second land-

'Dig For Victory' campaign poster issued by UK Ministry of Food in 1939.

Your Food in War-time', Cover of *Public Information Leafleat* no. 4,
London: Lord Privy Seal's Office, 1939 (15 million copies printed).

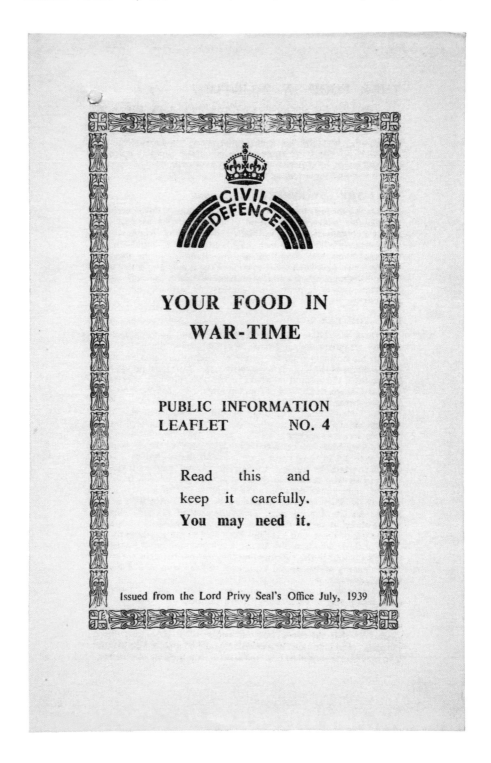

scape of man.[4] Clement never uses the term 'ecology' as he prefers to stress the autonomous power of the neglected and uncultivated spaces of the environment. Yet not even in a global megalopolis is the dominion of concrete absolute. A recent example of metropolitan resistance – guerrilla gardening and seed bombing – shows how cities are not a separate ecosystem but a terrain still permeable to 'involuntary' vegetation.

From ancient barbarians to modern biopolitics, war has changed (its) nature. The pacified and all-reconciling political horizon of *sustainability* brings to mind a war time without war, the siege of a silent Ghost Army.[5] Indeed it is more realistic to suppose, along the lines of contemporary political thought, that there is no longer an outside enemy. Within the field of *sustainable development* we have established the borders of our own siege.[6] Today's sustainability and 'consume less' imperatives are in fact shared by a broad spectrum of abiders from anarchist squatters to Prince Charles of Wales.[7] What were once collective coordinates of conflict are now individually introjected and de-politicized. The patriotic war *for* surplus has moved from the *home front* to the *inner front* to become a war *on* surplus, through a highly individualized calculation of energy consumption, carbon footprint, CO_2 emissions, intake of animal proteins, and so forth. The mantra 'consume less' echoes something of a born again Protestant ethics: 'Desire less.' A biopolitical governance has exerted its control once again from the midst of a so-called radical agenda.[8] In an unconscious way, urban farming and sustainable development resurrect the spectres of war and siege.

4. Gilles Clément, *Manifeste du Tiers Paysage* (Paris: Éditions Sujet/Objet, 2004).

5. The Ghost Army was a US Army tactical deception unit during the Second World War. It was given the unique mission to impersonate other army units in order to fool the enemy, using inflatable tanks and artillery, sound trucks, phoney radio transmissions and even playacting.

6. See: Michael Hardt and Antonio Negri, *Empire* (Cambridge, MA: Harvard University Press, 2000). Negri has recently criticized in particular the forms of *soft activism* in the metropolis which believe to easily escape the 'biopolitical diagram' of capitalism: experiments of urban farming included. See: A. Negri, et al., 'Qu'est-ce qu'un événement ou un lieu biopolitique dans la métropole?', in: *Multitudes #38: Une micropolitique de la ville: l'agir urbain* (Paris: Editions Amsterdam, 2008).

7. See: Amir Djalali (with Piet Vollaard), 'The Complex History of Sustainability', in: *Volume #18: After Zero* (Amsterdam: Archis Publisher, 2008).

8. Critiques *à la* Žižek about an 'ecology without nature' do not suffice in providing an alternative account of the *bios* and dismiss the spontaneous life of the 'third landscape'. See: Timothy Morton, *Ecology without Nature: Rethinking Environmental Aesthetics* (Cambridge, MA: Harvard University Press, 2007).

Hunting Swans and Stewing Tulips: The Netherlands under Occupation, 1943-1944

During the Second World War, another pamphlet that was widely distributed in the UK instructed civilians how to 'Eat for Victory'.[9] But this *homeland security* cuisine was simply addressing a more Spartan domestic economy and neglected the untapped surplus of edibles in the city, which other parts of Europe more devastated by war, such as the Netherlands, were forced to recognize. In non-war periods, edibles from the residual and unclean spaces of the city are considered indecent. Many schools of ecology, in particular, maintain a reverence for a 'wild' environment untouched by humans outside the urban border. On the contrary, there is always a spontaneous surplus of edibles in the city exceeding civic ecology, food distribution channels and activist urban farming. In violating the usual food chain, war uncovers the city as an organism in itself: the city 'becomes edible' but, moreover, starts to cannibalize itself: *urbanibalism*.

9. Jill Norman, *Eating For Victory: Healthy Home Front Cooking on War Rations* (London: Michael O'Mara, 2007).

The Dutch famine of 1944-1945, the so-called 'hunger winter', was precipitated by a railway strike in September 1944. The Nazis retaliated by placing an embargo on all food transports to the Netherlands. The war of attrition affected the country's Western provinces, the Randstad, most severely. Thousands of inhabitants were forced to rummage for fuel and food. Kitchens became makeshift laboratories as women and men experimented in turning livestock feed into digestible pap and sugar beets into *slagcrème* and stew.[10]

Due to the suspension of the country's flower exports, the tulip industry in West Holland had accumulated mountains of bulbs in storage. When the medical authorities announced that the high starch content of the bulbs made them edible, farmers set about selling their stockpiles as food. The local *Commission Concerning Household Information and Family Management* released a handbill advising the ways to prepare tulip bulbs as a soup, mash or biscuits. Not only did the bulbs require less cooking and prove to be tastier than sugar beets, the tulip bulb itself became the symbol of the hunger winter, and, in a sense, a patriotic provender.

10. Translaton of *whipped cream*, a culinary euphemism for a by-product of sugar beet. *Slagcrème* was popular as it looked delicious and suppressed hunger.

As the *hongerwinter* wore on, and the desperation rose, the Amsterdam populace became adept at hunting *urban game* – cats, dogs, horses, pigeons, even seagulls. As an eight-year-old, Frans

Lavell recounts how a children's story of a medieval king feasting on swan prompted his grandfather to catch swan in Amsterdam's Zuiderzeepark. Lavell's tale narrates the duo's cumbersome attempt to kill a swan who defended itself and his comrades even when headless: 'By golly, that beast was strong! Give me 30 of those swans and I'll drive all the Germans out of the Sarphatie street barracks!'[11] As with the tulip bulb – an emblem of Dutch capital – the hunted swan was a re-appropriation of a national symbol. Eating tulip or swan was not merely a matter of survival, but an act of insurgent culinary art.

11. Frans Lavell, 'Kerstzwaan', self-published article, 2008.

In Amsterdam, as in many other parts of Europe, war had divulged an unknown potential, a hidden *third landscape of food,* to again borrow Clément's concept.[12] Instead of designing sustainable gardens, Clément practices a spontaneous relation with the living residues of nature around us. His maps highlight interstices, borders and parasitic surfaces of the cityscape. He is concerned about opening *biological doors* and *corridors* between these residues to make biodiversity circulate informally across the city. Yet, what Clément does not consider are the edibles, the spontaneous sources of food that grow autonomously from any planned agriculture (the second landscape). Correspondingly, we propose urbanibalism as the *third landscape of food*, a practice of opening up *culinary corridors* that traverse the different *Umwelts* of urban life.

12. In recent decades, the Netherlands have cultured an impressive lineage of publications covering different facets of urban ecosystems. See: Ton Denters, *Stadsplanten: veldgids voor de stad* ('s Graveland: Fontaine uitgevers, 2004); Johan van Zoest and Martin Melchers, *Leven in de stad: Betekenis en toepassing van natuur in de stedelijke omgeving* (Utrecht: Uitgeverij Knvv, 2006); Martin Melchers and Geert Timmermans, *Haring in het IJ: De verborgen dierenwereld van Amsterdam* (Amsterdam: Stadsuitgeverij, 1991); and Remco Daalder, *Stadse Beesten* (Amsterdam: Lubberhuizen, 2005).

Aside from warfare, it is water that has been the prime enemy of the Netherlands. The Dutch environment has been 'made' by winning land from the sea, and this degree of 'artificiality' could also be said to be true of its culinary tradition. Yet, the country's state-of-the-art engineering, its hydrological system of pumping water from the arable polders will not be sufficient against the rising sea level. If climate change predictions are correct, the Randstad soil will be increasingly infiltrated by water. In anticipation of this transition, the Rotterdam-based firm Van Bergen Kolpa architects has imagined an entire new food ecosystem and a new culinary view of the Netherlands.[13] Rather than 'defensive' interventions of a mechanized agriculture, Van Bergen Kolpa proposes small-scale dynamic farming for a landscape with more frequent exchanges of salt and sweet waters between sea, lagoons, dunes, creeks and polders. Its 2040

13. Van Bergen Kolpa Architects, 'Food and the Randstad Metropolis', in: *Volume #18*, op. cit. (note 7).

Type-written fact sheet on the nutritional value of tulips (50 per cent greater than potatoes) and five recipes: two for tulip bulb mash pot and one each for soup, fried bulbs, and tulip bulbs as a binding ingredient. The hand-written note reads: '6. Roast them in the oven like chestnuts.' Courtesy Verzetsmuseum Amsterdam

TULPEN

Voedingswaarde: Hieromtrent deelt de Heer Dr.H.Varekamp arts te Oestgeest het volgende mede;
De voedingswaarde is zeer groot, ongeveer 50% hooger dan van aardappelen. Er heerscht eenig vooroordeel tegen het gebruik van tulpenbollen daar men aanvankelijk meende, dat er giftige bestanddeelen in zouden voorkomen. Het is echter gebleken dat dit niet het geval is en dat tulpenbollen geheel onschadelijk voor de gezondheid zijn.

Schoonmaken en bereiding; Achtereenvolgens worden bast en krans van de bol afgehaald, daarna snijdt men de bol overlangs door en haalt er de gele pit uit. De tulpenbollen worden op dezelfde wijze gekookt als aardappelen met dit verschil, dat ze in 7 minuten 15 à 20 m. gaar zijn. In droogen toestand blijven tulpen goed tot plm. 15 Februari.

Recepten.
1. stampot met tulpenbollen.Men neme b.v. 2 K.G. tulpenbollen 2 K.G. aardappelen en 4 K.G. roode kool. De bollen worden afzonderlijk gekookt, de aardappelen met de roode kool. Daarna de stampot met de bollen afmaken met een weinig zout en specerijen op smaak brengen.

2. Stampot met zuurkool. Men neme b.v. 2 K.G. schoon gemaakte bollen en 1½ K.G. zuurkool. Bollen en zuurkool gelijktijdig gaar koken, daarna met zout en specerijen afmaken.

3. Soep. Men neme b.v. 2 K.G. bollen, deze schoonmaken, gaar koken, water afgieten, daarna stampen en met 5 Liter water verdunnen. Soepgroenten bijvoegen en naar smaak zout en specerijen.

4. Gebakken tulpenbollen. Schoongemaakte, als uien gesneden tulpenbollen zijn te gebruiken als versnaperingen. Men snippert deze als uien in de frituur en laat ze lichtbruin aanfruiten.

5. Bindmiddel. Wordt op dezelfde wijze gemaakt als bindmiddel van aardappelen. (kan lang bewaard worden)

6 Poffen in de oven als tamme Kastanjes (Emmy)

Flow Food menu shows the culinary potential of a wetter climate: a salad of barley with Dutch marsh herbs including watercress, wild chives, dandelion leaves, water mint; saddle of lamb with parsnip and sea lavender; oysters in an aspic of seawater and agar with *Salicornia* seagrass. The *third landscape of food* of the Netherlands will demand a new culinary art.

'And They Ate the Zoo.' Paris Commune under Siege, 1870-1871

Not all sieges are about starvation only. Some have also proven to be a creative, rebellious, joyful and decadent *expansion of the edible*, as was the case on the barricades of the Paris Commune fighting against the Prussians in 1870-1871. Parisians were gastronomically curious, 'involved in a process of discovery, and of creation', writes Rebecca Spang.[14] The forced *urbanibalism* of the siege was clearly enriched and reinvented by a sophisticated culinary tradition to 'spiritualize matter' and to transform the edible into, respectively, an aesthetic experience, a passionate topic of conversation and, not least, a political gesture. A cartoon of a Montmartre butcher's shop selling cat, rat and dog meat in Paris 1871 displays, however, a less noble phenomenon: 'It is estimated that during the siege over 5000 cats were slaughtered and eaten. A young cat, it was found; tasted like a squirrel but was tenderer and sweeter.'[15]

14. Rebecca L. Spang, 'And They Ate the Zoo: Relating Gastronomic Exoticism in the Siege of Paris', *MLN*, no. 4, vol. 107 (September 1992) French Issue.

15. *Current Opinion #4* (New York: Current Literature Pub. Co, 1890), 379. For a diaristic account of horse, dog, cat and rat meat eaten during the siege, see: Nathan Sheppard, *Shut Up in Paris* (London: Richard Bentley and Son, 1871).

The most legendary, baroque and pantagruelian event was the sacrifice of the elephants Castor and Pollux of the zoo at the Jardin des Plantes. The dramatic end of the elephants was recorded in the last days of December 1870 in the *Gazette des Absents*, a twice-weekly periodical published during the siege and delivered by balloon to avoid the encircling Prussian forces. A restaurant menu from 25 December, the 99th day of the siege, offered *Consommé d'Eléphant* together with *Cuissot de Loup, sauce Chevreuil* (haunch of wolf with a deer sauce), *Terrine d'Antilope aux truffes* (terrine of antelope with truffles), *Civet de Kangourou* (kangaroo stew) and *Chameau rôti à l'anglaise* (roasted camel, English style). Of course, the poorest Parisians did not benefit from the decision to 'eat the zoo' and there was no real urgency to do so. In fact, some butchers started to speculate by selling horse meat as the exclusive elephant meat, thus only apparently replacing the more traditional *hippophagie*.[16]

16. Spang, 'And They Ate the Zoo', op. cit. (note 14). *Hippophagie* is French for eating horse meat.

Auguste Charpentier, *Rat ayant servi à l'alimentation pendant le siège de Paris, 15 janvier, 1871* (A Sewer Rat served as food during the Siege of Paris). Courtesy Musée Carnavalet, Paris

The study of animals eaten in times of war deserves a new discipline, something between *polemozoology* and *polemogastronomy* (whereas the more 'conventional' *polemobotany* is devoted to research how flora is spread and affected by war). This discipline would have been crucial at the time of Paris siege. As Spang puts it: 'For fifty years before the siege, gastronomic guides (written to help the eater become "a clever tactician" prepared to do "combat" with the restaurateur) concentrated on the question of correctly identifying the component parts of a dish. The skilled eater, likened to Adam in the Garden of Eden, excelled in giving the one true name to a dish. The siege, then, demonstrated the eater's finest hour. In December of 1870, to name a dish correctly is also to call an animal by name. "Fantastical cookery" whether practiced, anticipated or discussed gave material substance both to meals and to conversations.'

The siege expanded the range of edible 17. Ibid.
matter so much that it transmutated also those trades and commodities that usually dealt with the realm of *non-food*. As trade outside the city becomes impossible, Paris merchants exchange functions among themselves; every shopkeeper becomes a grocer. Hairdressers and silversmiths sell poultry in 'a singular transmutation of commerce and a bizarre transfiguration of boutiques'. Yet nothing indicates that hunger might completely obliterate the specialization of stores and of goods. In these texts, the siege means not starvation but the expansion of the edible, the saleable and the noteworthy. A parfumeur's stock expands to include 'more or less de-perfumed oils' (butter substitutes) while it remains in the realm of the olfactory by offering herring and onions.[18] 18. Ibid.

This radical and inventive cuisine was also claimed by the workers' movement, which demanded not simply food to survive in time of war, but food for a modern revolution and the culinary pleasure as a constituent and materialistic right of the communards themselves. In his gastronomic novel *La vivandiera di Montélimar*, Gianni-Emilio Simonetti highlighted the emancipated role of the women of the Commune – proto-feminists fighting on the frontline of both the culinary and military barricades.[19] The siege of Paris also prompted the *légumiste* Élisée Reclus, a renowned geographer and anarchist advocating a meat-free diet as a form of rebellion and pioneer of the animal rights movement.

19. See: Gianni-Emilio Simonetti, *La vivandiera di Montélimar: Il secolo delle rivolte logiche e la nascita della cucina moderna nelle memorie di una pétroleuse* (Rome: Derive Approdi, 2004).

Which culinary movement is the urban landscape calling for? Contemporary aesthetics such as food design, molecular cuisine

Menu of a Paris restaurant featuring 'consommé d'éléphant', roasted camel and other animals allegedly from the zoo. Date reads 25 December 1870, '99th day of siege'. Courtesy Archives François de la Jousselinière, Paris

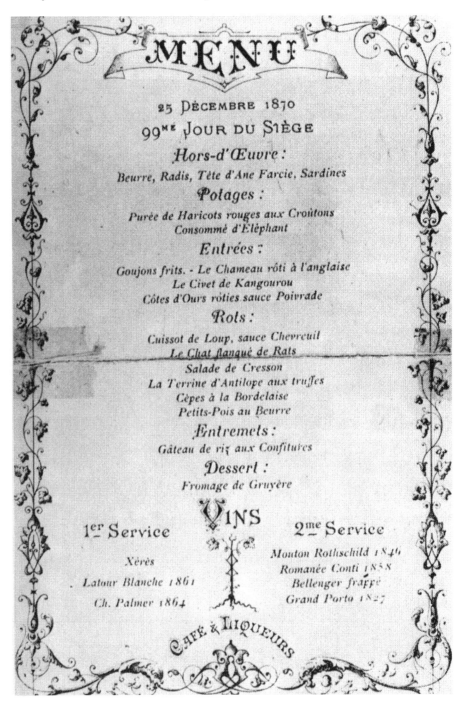

and bioart are only seemingly innovative and poor on the ecological ground since they mainly render food as an object of engineering or genetic code for programming. They only touch the surface of the edible and never its living matter (nothing is less spontaneous than bioart playing with DNA). In this sense, ancient recipes, the recent Slow Food presidia or *urbanibalism* in times of war may incarnate a more comprehensive 'scientific' knowledge than the techno-determinism of the latest biotech patent. Both techno-fetishist cuisine as well as eco-asceticism remove the *bios* as a living, flourishing and fermenting substance.

Opposite a pedestrian vitalism, the French philosopher Michel Serres reminds us of the dystopian dimension of nature in his book *The Parasite*. Nature is but a never-ending chain of parasites eating each other down to the invisible ones: 'The fruit spoils, the milk sours, the wine turns into vinegar, the vegetables rot, the stores of wheat are filled with rats and weevils. Everything ferments, everything rots. Everything changes.'[20] Microorganisms take our body back to nature after death: putrefaction is life, too. An unseen world of bacteria, fungi and yeasts is also part of our daily diet: they breath with us and eat with us (in our intestinal tract).

20. Michel Serres, *Le Parasite* (Paris: Grasset, 1980); translation: *The Parasite* (Baltimore: Johns Hopkins University Press, 1982), 156-183.

Beer and bread are different across Europe precisely because the microflora are different everywhere and especially within the city. The know-how and the alliance with this microscopic and ever-proliferating world of parasites is what made humanity win the war against many viruses and noxious bacteria. Yeast was likely the divine agent [!] that made the miracle of turning the water into wine and gave us a new life, according to Serres: '[Ambrosia] is the brew that saved the human population of the Fertile Crescent, and from even further East of Eden, from certain infectious diseases found in the lakes and backwaters. Beer, wine, and bread, foods of fermentation, of bubbling, foods of decay, appeared as safeguards against death. These were our first great victories over parasites, our rivals . . . From the Olympians to the Last Supper, we have celebrated the victory to which we owe our life, the eternity of phylogenesis, and we celebrated it in its natural spot, the table.'[21]

21. Ibid.

Cities always ferment, nations too. Yet the cult of an ever-expanding *life* has also had its fair share of dangerous and identitarian interpretations which formed the basis of Nazi ideology. Hitler's notion of *Lebensraum* (literally 'living space') served as a major justification for Germany's aggression in East Europe to procure land and raw materials for a *Großdeutschland*. The urban population was to be exterminated by starvation, thus creating an agricultural surplus to feed Germany.

Ferment Brussels: A Toast to Communal Forms of Life, Brussels 2030

If a conclusion is to be drawn, it should be a recipe embracing the practices of *urbanibalism* as a valuable contravention to the upcoming forms of national conflict in Northwestern Europe. This recipe is located in Brussels, a fitting destination and nodal point of a journey between the Dutch *hongerwinter* and the siege of the Paris Commune, along the debated split between Wallonia and Flanders and alongside the gastronomic faultline between Mediterranean and Nordic cultures.

Ferment Brussels is an urban hydromiel, or *ambrosia* (the same mythological drink of Greek gods and first alcoholic beverage of early humankind): a therapeutic potion and a source of alcohol made from ingredients collected within the metropolitan landscape and from its invisible microflora. It is easily prepared by mixing one part of water with two parts of urban honey.[22] This concoction is then fermented with an infusion of plants: average city plant roots such as shepard's-purse, thistle or burdock can be used. All ingredients are then combined, heated and poured into a large glass vat with an airlock for four weeks. Fermentation should start within the first 24 hours, or can be precipitated by inoculating the wort with a few drops of local beer (Brussels has a particular type of beer, the Lambic, which fits this recipe, as it is spontaneously fermented by an indigenous urban yeast called *Brettanomyces brux-ellensis*).[23] To get a fizzy and modern ambrosia, *Ferment Brussels* can be put into a resilient soda bottle for one week to turn fermentation into a very dense and delicate foam. Within the bottle, the invisible 'social ferment' of Brussels turns the urban honey into a convivial alcoholic beverage.

22. Urban honey is surprisingly non-polluted: in processing nectar into honey, bees eliminate any pollutants. Also, there are more bees in cities compared to the countryside, because of the herbicides used in agriculture. See the beekeeping project and purity analysis made by Marc Wollast at www.apisbruocsella.be.

23. We used a Lambic made at the Brasserie Cantillon (www.cantillon.be). For more details of this recipe see: www.urbanibalism.org.

The Latin term for feast, *convivium,* literally means 'living together': eating together as communal life. *Convivium* can be more extensively understood as the 'commons of the living things' (as in *herbarium* or *bestiarium*). The dimension of the *convivium* should be more important than the restrained and individual production of any ecologically correct urban farming. What green capitalism

Air-locked vessel fermenting the 'Ferment Brussels' hydromiel.
Temperature is controlled by a desk lamp connected to a
thermostat inside an unused fridge. Amsterdam, October 2008
(www.urbanibalism.org).

will never be keen to share is the profit which will be accumulated on the new soils of sustainable agriculture and renewable energies. The first-ever alcoholic drink of humankind is offered here as a memento of the very remote past and very remote future, as a toast to insurgent and communal forms of life. This ambrosia is dedicated against the possible split of Belgium and to the impossible split of the ecosystem, to the invisible and flourishing world of creatures that are part of our daily food, wellbeing and inebriated states of mind, in particular, to all of us – invisible producers of surplus-value for the upcoming regime of green capitalism.

book reviews

Matteo Pasquinelli
*Animal Spirits: A Bestiary
of the Commons*

Willem van Weelden

Rotterdam, NAi Publishers in
association with the Institute of
Network Cultures, Hogeschool
van Amsterdam, 2008,
ISBN 978-90-5662-663-1,
240 pp., € 19.50

Twenty years after the introduction of the postmodern 'delirium', the notion launched by Jean Baudrillard in his famous thriller *Fatal Strategies*, the problem of finding a diagnosis of our times and a cultural critique that is not the victim of the many-headed monster of 'hyperreality' is still urgent. Baudrillard introduced the term in order to point out the loss of our ability to describe reality simply yet in all its fullness. Inspired by Marshall McLuhan, he supported his theory by emphasizing that the nature of human relationships is determined by the forms of communication employed. But this very fact opens the way to what is ultimately a self-referential way of thinking which, in the final analysis, only problematicizes one's own choices and orientations. Society as a functioning whole can only be indirectly understood as a self-referential framework ending in the zero degree of its own thought. This methodical problem, this 'aporia', still seems to exert a traditional weight on the shoulders of the writer and researcher Matteo Pasquinelli, whose *Animal Spirits: A Bestiary of the Commons* is a brave attempt at throwing

off the historical burden and escaping from this theoretical narcosis and melancholy.

But it would be silly to judge this unusual book solely on whether this escape has succeeded, since Pasquinelli rummages through a lot more. What makes the book special is that it uses the concept of the bestiary (even though only three animals are presented) to provide an ideological critique of the culture industry and of what is currently happening in network culture, such as the media landscape of terrorist warfare and Internet porn. The book moreover attempts to provide an answer to the question as to how this analysis could be used to think about the establishment of a digital commons. To be perfectly clear, Pasquinelli sees the commons as a broad social given, and not just as Creative Commons, an alternative concept for copyright. He starts out from a more general idea of a common as a way of basing issues regarding property or deriving rights not on traditional market thinking but on openness, communality and shared responsibility – in short, on a new sociality. *Animal Spirits* should therefore be seen

primarily as an affirmative political study of the conditions that would contribute to such an endeavour.

In order to give a good description of the arena in which the struggle over the commons is being fought, he opens with an appeal to take as a guiding principle the 'animal spirit' that he sees everywhere in network culture. Borrowing from the theories of John Maynard Keynes, who saw in this animal spirit precisely the unpredictable human driving force of economic cycles, and in line with the recent work of the neo-neo-Marxist Paulo Virno (see the interview with Virno in *Open* nr. 17), Pasquinelli advocates a revision of the theoretical perspective. The dirtiness and brutality and intrinsic conflict of today's network reality should be taken seriously as a precondition and not be theoretically, aesthetically or rhetorically glossed over under the unction of good intentions, sterile utopias of horizontality and the celebration of the paradigm 'information wants to be free'. He sets against this credo of the Free Culture movement the hard, material reality that might or might not provide us with access to some culture or other, and points out that the accumulation of information simultaneously nourishes forms of speculation and new communication monopolies. For Pasquinelli, thinking about a common also therefore implies an investigation into the broader material impact and consequences of the deployment of cultural capital.

In his elaboration of this conceptual programme he then deals with three phantasmagoric monsters: the managerial parasite (derived from Michel Serres's *The Parasite*) of the digital commons, the hydra (a mythical many-headed, dragon-like snake) of the cleansing of the 'creative cities', and the double-headed eagle of power and desire that governs the media landscape of war and porn. For him, the parasite stands for the completely parasitical relationships that have taken over the production of knowledge in cognitive capitalism, whereby work, politics and art are inextricably entangled and mutual dependence and exploitation are the rule – a circumstance that seriously blocks the creation of a healthy political opposition or conflict. Conflict is completely watered down in accordance with the micro-politics of relationships of dependence.

The culture of 'dog eats dog' runs rampant. According to Pasquinelli, there is no room for a naive trust in the inherent goodness of the human species. He sees Web 2.0 as offering no utopian guarantee that the horizontality of knowledge production will turn out for the good, although he does not exclude this as a possibility, as long as we are aware of the animal machinations. A powerful example that he uses to analyse these machinations, one which in his view represents the ultimate basis of the knowledge economy, is the enormous increase in property speculation, which is the material shadow of the 'creative commons'. After 20 years of ideological misunderstandings and two years of credit crisis, says Pasquinelli, we now have a chance of abolishing the longstanding asymmetry between the squatters movement and Internet activism. The crisis in the financial markets is ensuring both the collapse of the symbolic, immaterial value which manifests itself online and a physical depreciation in the property market, for example. Pasquinelli sees a chance here for achieving a communal creative sabotage of the system, which can be used to provide a contribution to a common – at a symbolic, representative and material level.

Despite these fruitful theoretical interventions and ardent appeals for practical analysis and action, there's still something that doesn't gel. Pasquinelli wants to do too much within too short a scope, which means that his insights are not thoroughly thought out. You can already sense this at the beginning of the book – you keep searching in the introduction for the eventual position assumed by Pasquinelli, and for what he actually has in his sights in his analysis of the zoo of *Animal Spirits*. With elegance and inventiveness he jumps into the theoretical dance around the right way to view the abysses of previous failures and excesses, but in this breakdance he reveals too little faith in his own bestial right, and the connection between theoretical insight and materialistic elaboration is not completely satisfactory. His *Animal Spirits* is not quite the moving body of a new political practice. That is certainly no easy ambition, and Pasquinelli can only be commended for having made this *salto bestiale*. At any rate, it's a real relief that we again have a funky book to get excited about, with or without a *Potere Operaismo* 2.0 as decor.

Ed Romein, Marc
Schuilenburg en Sjoerd
van Tuinen (ed.)
Deleuze Compendium

Amsterdam, Boom, 2009,
ISBN: 9789085065388,
408 pp., € 29.90

Kathleen Vandeputte

Although the philosophy of Gilles Deleuze has long been influential, not only in philosophical, but also in academic, artistic and political circles, a thorough survey of his work has been lacking in Dutch-speaking regions. This need has in any case been met with the publication of the *Deleuze Compendium*. As Deleuze's appealing, dandyish gaze on the cover leads us to suspect, his idiosyncratic philosophy leaves few unmoved. An understanding of his thinking, however, is not so self-evident and pretty much goes hand in hand with a solid and difficult read. A guidebook aimed at putting his philosophy into perspective would therefore certainly be no luxury.

The compendium takes us through an effervescent Deleuzian landscape of differential virtuality, rhizomatic planes of immanence and nomadic streams of desire. It is a philosophy for travelling in, with expert guides like Isabelle Stengers, Henk Oosterling and Rudi Laermans, to mention a few. Yet whoever thinks that they can get away with an easy-going, all-in trip will be misled. In Deleuze's work we come up against a recalcitrant philosophy that leaves many a reader perplexed. His writings are riddled with concepts such as rhizomatic, endo-consistency, noology, chaosmos and – to mention one

more – indi-drama-different/ciation. Are not the most interesting philosophers those who invent and reconfigure concepts because their ravishing thought happens to run up against the limits of language? The importance of Deleuze reaches further than just an appreciation of postmodern eclecticism or fashionable 'geneologizing'; his thinking arises out of a current necessity and concrete problems in philosophy, since it reveals something of reality. This is crystallized in his side-swipe at the terror of self-satisfied thinking and his constant renewal of concepts in order to deploy them in his own philosophy. But this does not by any means imply an intellectual demolition through putting paid once and for all to the philosophical tradition. His early work, with monographs on Hume, Nietzsche, Bergson and Spinoza, which are dealt with in the first part of the compendium, bears witness to this. In the French climate around 1950, when the voices of Hegel, Heidegger and Husserl were reverberating the loudest, Deleuze's decision to interpret exactly these philosophers can at least be called daring and unconventional. This becomes clear in the essay by Romein, in which Hume is given a figurative transcendental-empirical interpretation, and in the piece by Peter de Graeve, where

Deleuze's specific interpretation of Nietzsche leads to the development of the notion of 'conceptual personages'.

In the second part we are introduced to the shift towards a particular development of his body of ideas, with often complicated books such as *Le pli*, *Différence et répetition* and *Logique du sens*. In contrast to the melancholy that disillusioned Marxists seem to propagate, Deleuze brings a new dynamism to philosophy by making curiosity and original creation the driving force of thinking, but without falling into naive optimism or experimental pottering. Ger Groot confirms this dynamism in his piece about differentiation: 'Those who really think must dare to abandon the evidentiality, clarity and apparent irrefutability that offer the mind safety and security' (page 144).

The third part discusses his collaboration with Felix Guatarri and their two-volume *Capitalisme et Schizophrénie*. Marx, Freud and Nietzsche, the masters of mistrust, accompany them in their critique of the logic of identity and representation and of desire as a fundamental lack, although Deleuze and Guattari also think beyond May '68, as Laermans subtly demonstrates. Deleuze's excursions into other domains (mostly art, but also ontology, mathematics and physics), which is focussed on in the last part, point to the broad strength of Deleuze's ideas. In the words of Sarah Posman in her compelling piece about literature and the stuttering of language: 'It is a bastard perspective that sends your thinking in directions that you would not have thought possible' (page 299).

It would be un-Deleuzian not to get cracking oneself in a dissipative way with Deleuze's framework of concepts, just as a presentation of his philosophy as an absolute transparent system would not be in keeping with the nature and style of his thinking. Any attempt at this would just get bogged down in what Deleuze disputes: the reduction of philosophical thinking to a homogeneous, clichéd essence registered in the philosophophological *clarté*. This means, in other words, that philosophy must be perpetrated and not simply studied in order to be followed. The compendium succeeds astonishingly well in providing pieces of the puzzle here and there, which even make you hungry in advance for further reading. The occasional repetitions that the book perforce contains are not disturbing in the least; rather, they rhizomize through the reading of the book, so that one becomes more strongly tied and compelled to an affective bond with differentiating, Deleuzian process thinking. One and the same theme is folded open from different perspectives as

a 'regaining. permeated with difference and deviation, of the singular' (page 125). In particular, the introductory essay by the editors immediately manages in this way to be exciting, just as Oosterling's 'Rhizome', Schuilenburg's 'Assemblages' and Marcel Cobussen also further elaborate on the theme of the rhizomatic. This perspectivism is formally stressed because the essays do not presume an imperative sequence of reading meant to lead to a systematic accumulation of knowledge. Most of the essays challenge, although not always explicitly, the various critiques that weigh on Deleuze's work: from Badiou's reproach that behind the multiplicity there still lies hidden a melancholic *Sehnsucht* for the One (in, among others, the essay by Wiep van Bunge and Leen de Bolle) to the sceptical critique that the glorification of continual 'becoming' and 'creating' connects seamlessly with capitalist consumerism (dealt with in the essay, for example, by Patricia Pisters and Laermans). On the contrary, such a picture of Deleuze is alien to this book.

Deleuze's philosophizing, in which thinking is fundamentally connected with immanence, sets us firmly back with two feet on the ground after an interminable period dominated by a Platonic and Cartesian tradition. Here the influence of Spinoza and phenomenology is indisputable, as the lucid essays by Wiep van Bunge and

Judith Wambacq respectively make clear. Transcendance and dualism are radically put paid to, while his rebelliousness and Nietzschean distrust of a hegemony of thinking stimulate creativity. Yet this unbridled creativity perhaps rather gets in the way of the accessibility and lucidity that this compendium speaks of. The density of Deleuze's work seems to repeat itself in a number of essays, so that the reader ends up feeling lost in the academic constructions ventured in Van Tuinen's *Le pli*, for example, or when Richard de Brabander, in his essay on Foucault, discusses the grafting of archaeology onto geology, and now and then in Ils Huygens's essay 'Cinema'. Nevertheless, this compendium paves the way to Deleuze's work itself, since in its many-sidedness it manages to affect.

The fact that Deleuze ceaselessly questions the dominant doxa of the present, thereby indicating the symptoms of contemporary philosophical discourse, points to his difficult and non-contemporary thinking. That he also adulates openness and uncertainty in thinking makes him not only an indispensable philosopher but also – and perhaps more importantly – a thinker whom we want to 'read out of love'.[1]

1. Gilles Deleuze, *Pourparlers* (Paris, Éditions de Minuit, 1990), 16.

Nicolas Bourriaud
The Radicant

Ilse van Rijn

New York, Sternberg Press,
2009,
ISBN: 978-1-933128-42-9,
192 pp., €15.00

More than ten years after the publication of his much discussed book *Esthétique relationnelle* (1998), the English translation of which, *Relational Aesthetics* (2002), appeared at about the same time as his subsequent essay, *Postproduction* (2001), Nicolas Bourriaud has now published *The Radicant*. The book was written between 2005 and 2007 in the various cities he was living in: Paris, Venice, Kiev, Madrid, Havana, New York, Moscow, Turin and finally London. Bourriaud recently organized the Tate Triennial in London (3 February – 26 April 2009), which he christened 'Altermodern'. As we can in the meantime expect from Bourriaud, this title, like that of the present book, is more than just the name of a project. Once again, the curator who writes as well as travels is using his collaboration with artists to descry a phenomenon that needs to be named and elevated to a new category. The theory of 'relational aesthetics' was developed in connection with 'Traffic', the exhibition which he organized in 1996 in CapcMusée d'art contemporaine in Bordeaux. Now, too, we see theory taking shape in close dialogue with practice. The current juncture can be typified as 'altermodern', says Bourriaud – our way of thinking and living displays 'radicant' patterns. In *The Radicant*, Bourriaud takes a closer look at these two, inter-related concepts.

The book consists of three parts: a theoretical account of 'Altermodernity', an aesthetic reflection based on works of art under the heading 'Radicant Aesthetics' and an elaboration of his 'radicant ideas' relating to cultural production and contemporary means of consumption and use, this chapter being called 'Treatise on Navigation'.

Bourriaud states the importance of reconsidering modernity. Twentieth century modernism was dominated by radical movements in which artists returned time and time again to the roots of art or of society, in an attempt to purify an origin or rediscover essences. Bourriaud, however, is now waging that the modernity of our century will be discovered in contrast to such radicalism, yet without any attempt at whitewashing a standardization of the imagination set in motion by globalization. Today's makers are establishing the basis for this art of the future, which he calls 'radicant'. 'Radicant' is a botanical term for organisms whose roots form new roots while growing. It will not escape most people's notice that this sprouting root has a lot in common with that other metaphor derived from botany, the rhizome. Whereas Deleuze and Guattari's fluid, non-hierarchical structure places the subject between brackets already from the outset, Bourriaud maintains that

with the radicant the subject is implicit. The radicant assumes the form of a path or a trajectory; the radicant subject carries his roots along with him on his travels and questions them. With the result that: 'To be radicant means setting one's roots in motion, staging them in heterogeneous contexts and formats, denying them the power to completely define one's identity, translating ideas, transcoding images, transplanting behaviours, exchanging rather than imposing.' In response to this radicant art, Bourriaud calls today's modernity a global equivalent of and an alternative to the historical period – an 'altermodernity'.

'Altermodernity' distances itself from the postmodern reaction to modernism which, says Bourriaud, has bred standardization. While postmodern multiculturalism did little more than stimulate cultural anchoring and ethnic enrootedness through promoting a respectful inclination towards 'the other', Bourriaud concludes that no 'others' exist today. There are only other places ('elsewheres'). This statement, which represents an important argument within Bourriaud's general theory, is partly based on the writings of Victor Segalen, the traveller and Symbolist-inspired poet who, at the beginning of the twentieth century, expressed his ideas about man's relationship to his environment in notes that were later published under the title *Essay* on Exotism: An Aesthetics of Diversity. Translated into the present time, 'neutral areas', concretized in airports and train stations, the result of globalization, can be regarded as temporary, precarious abodes, artificially created through a cultural mix that generates singularity. In these spaces, unmarked by a single, overpowering past ('smooth spaces'), artists carve a way of their own through a multiplicity of signs. Bourriaud calls them 'semionauts'. For him, the immigrant, the exile, the tourist and the 'urban wanderer' are the dominant figures within this contemporary culture. The question they pose is no longer: Where do you come from?, but: Where are you going to? There is room in these neutral spaces for discussions, dialogues and negotiations. What prevails here is an aesthetics of diversity.

The work of art is consistent with this dynamic, explains Bourriaud. It is 'time-specific', translating the condition of the one location into the other. In this way, translation counts as an important new artistic means. The altermodern work of art is characterized by its precarious status, its portability and its experimental form, as opposed to the modernistic constancy of permanent installations that were devised in terms of progress and constructive development.

Thomas Hirschhorn's temporary Monuments (to Deleuze and Spinoza, among others) can thus be regarded as radicant and altermodern. And, according to Bourriaud, the movement of the knights in Gabriel Orozco's *Knights Running Endlessly* (1995) is typical of a radicant aesthetics. In support of his ideas, works regularly crop up in *The Radicant* by artists familiar to us from his *Esthétique relationnelle* and *Postproduction*, such as Philippe Parreno, Rirkrit Tiravanija and Liam Gillick. But mention is also made of lesser-known artists whose works were included in 'Altermodern': Loris Gréaud and Spartacus Chetwynd, Seth Price, Subodh Gupta and Pascale Marthine Tayou. The question inevitably arises as to whether in *The Radicant* Bourriaud is once again preaching to the converted, a reproach that was levelled against him with regard to *Esthétique relationnelle*.

Clearly, a certain degree of distance is lacking in *The Radicant*. Sometimes this is less problematic than on other occasions. Bourriaud virtually identifies with Victor Segalen. Like Bourriaud himself, 'Segalen travels; he reports from the field'. The reference to this early theorist is inspiring, and adds value to The *Radicant*. But the lack of distance also typifies his theoretical 'conclusions'. Terms like 'radicant' and 'altermodern' seem no more than tendentious, temporary labels, name tags on a suitcase, while the intrinsic, theoretically sounded out basis for these fails to extend beyond its own borders. Bourriaud labelled the work of Philippe Parreno in the 1990s as a typical form of relational aesthetics, describes it a bit later as an example of *postproduction*, and now presents it as *the* form of radicant art showing us the way to an altermodern period. To posit such rapidly changing descriptions as conceptual categories does not help the credibility of Nicolas Bourriaud's theoretical 'reflections'. At most they can be seen as polemical stands.

Sven Lütticken
*Idols of the Market:
Modern Iconoclasm and
the Fundamentalist Spectacle*

Ilse van Rijn

New York, Sternberg Press,
2009,
ISBN: 978-1-933128-26-9, 248
pp., €19.00

With a view to historicizing iconoclasm to the point at which its potential for the current situation becomes visible, Sven Lütticken has collected five of his substantial essays under the title *Idols of the Market: Modern Iconoclasm and the Fundamentalist Spectacle*. He calls the book not only essayistic but also interventionist, rather than academic. In his introduction Lütticken provides a clear answer to the question of how, by means of a book, you can intervene in an issue that appears to have become delicate and complex in recent years: critical thinking is a necessary condition for intervention. However, the important thing is not to institutionalize this critique and at the same time to expose its inefficiency. Lütticken calls on us to think beyond the 'idols of the market'. It is more productive 'to re-imagine religion' than to fall back into a hysterical atheism as represented by the harsh criticism of the protest against images like the Danish cartoons which its opponents regard as both idolatrous and blasphemous. Western enlightenment thinking and a diabolical monotheism – particularly Islam – and the opposition to them are merely strengthened by such ruthless attitudes. Rethinking religion is facilitated by consciously creating overlaps, at present often still incidental, between academic, artistic and activist contexts, of which *Idols of the Market* is both a result and an example. Such collaborations also provide the freedom for the urgent reconsideration of the image.

In order to read the image anew, Lütticken concentrates in the five essays on contemporary forms of iconoclasm, while not eschewing philosophical, economic and theological 'excursions'. These digressions result in virtuoso texts in which the points are just as diverse as the sometimes unexpected references and turns. In the first essay, 'Myths of Iconoclasm', Lütticken touches on the few occasions that Islam and its protagonists are taken seriously in Western philosophy, varying from Montesquieu's *Lettres Persanes* to the writings of Hegel. He then goes on, via Nietzsche's views about God – the ex-parrot – whom Nietzsche declares to be dead rather than non-existent, to underpin the difference between 'mythos' and 'logos' and to point out the persistent existence of myth in Nietzsche himself. The ostensible revival of religion is a historical myth that expresses a social and cultural reality, Lütticken continues. The question is whether God is not a phantom, a sign and an invisible image that moves about in the media spectacle rather than in daily reality. Basing himself on Freud's *Moses and Monotheism*, he argues in response to his own question that physical iconoclasm has an equal in the spiritual, conceptual iconoclasm that was the domain of great thinkers and artists. Only a dialectics between these two variants of iconoclasm can bring about the dynamism that characterized great historical moments like the Reformation. It is because of this that the image could, and can, be defined once again. Today, says Lütticken, the work of Gert Jan Kocken testifies to such a dialectics. The enhanced materiality of Kocken's pictures leads to what Lütticken calls visual iconoclasm.

Although the path leading to this interim conclusion is sometimes dizzying and deliberately anachronistic, Lütticken's attempt at reading images differently never loses sight of the relevance of his amplifications for artistic and theoretical practice. And vice versa: What starting points, he asks himself, are offered by modern theory and art for mediating in the struggle between fundamentalisms?

Lütticken repeatedly stresses that the modern critique of the visual in art is not directed against images as such, but against instrumentalized visuality in regulated representations. Asger Jorn aimed at 'smashing the frame that suffocates the image', while the artist

Natascha Sadr Haghighian recently asked herself: How [does one] erase the images that create invisibilities? We can find an answer, writes Lütticken, in Sean Snyder's work 'From One Spectacle to Another'. Snyder suggests that a material analysis of representations cannot pass over the details within today's image production. Focussing on the use of photograph and video in the current 'War on Terror', he concludes that both the Pentagon and Al Qaida and kindred groups who produce, reproduce and distribute these images are hardly aware of the status of the image. It is up to artists like Snyder, thinks Lütticken, to reflect on this and to read the symptoms. After all, a symptom is a temporary trace of missed moments of liberation, such as revolutions or attempts at them, which can always be reactivated. Just as Snyder can perceive an image anew by means of a renewed encounter with it, so we should likewise reappropriate religion. Under the motto 'if there is a future . . . it has already happened' we can regard Paul and the early Christians as contemporaries, not because of their dogmas, but because of their unrelenting resistance to what is or has been.

As Lütticken writes at the beginning of his essay 'Attending to Things (Some More Material than Others)', we should reject the tendency to associate religion with fanaticism and a fleeing from the world. Are criticisms of idolatry and iconoclasm just symptoms of a transcendental aversion to material? Implicitly or explicitly, aesthetic thinking is always political, he emphasizes, following Rancière. Yet this proposition does not prevent the author of *Idols of the Market* from falling back on his pet subject, Marxism and later readings of it, in order to demonstrate the produced value of articles and of art works, however immaterial and conceptual these may be. What are ostensibly objects that speak for themselves, such as 'branded consumer goods', have to become 'things', 'matters of concern' that are open to discussion and, as such, can be produced and used 'differently'. Since 9/11, the 'West' and 'Islam' have been transformed into 'super brands', entrancing the consumers of the fundamentalist spectacle and turning them into slaves. What we have to do, says Lütticken, is 'turn the oppressive "facts" of life into forms'. Those sharing in this project can be called true representatives of the critique of idolatry. And of that of monotheism, should they so wish. Just as religion has its secular side, so is hypercapitalism not lacking in abstractions and every abstraction is more and more concretized today. Are these materializations of the immaterial becoming our current 'product[s] of thought'? A fully nuanced critique of the polarization between the West and Islam is revealed in the final chapter, 'Veiled Revelation'. Gestures of revelation are part of Enlightenment rhetoric, Lütticken reminds us. Whereas veiling, in its turn, betrays on the one hand a mystification – of women, social relationships and of Islam – the 'abstracting' robe is at the same time deployed in order to divulge liberal Western values, the West's seemingly unhindered emphasis on visibility. Paradoxically enough, veiling, like other iconoclastic gestures, creates new images which sometimes display a surprising similarity with aesthetic modernism, staging a spectacular representation of 'Otherness' in their game with visibility.

The 'excursions' that the author warned us of in his introduction turn out to be the points of entry that have enabled him to approach and differentiate a complex theme. *Idols of the Market: Modern Iconoclasm and the Fundamentalist Spectacle* is well supported with references and affirms Sven Lütticken as an intelligent and well-read writer who moreover incites new forms of collaboration between previously separate contexts, or what used to be known as opponents.

PERSONALIA

John Armitage teaches contemporary art and cultural theory in the Department of Visual Arts at Northumbria University in Great Britain. He is co-editor, with Ryan Bishop and Douglas Kellner, of the journal *Cultural Politics*, editor of *Virilio Live: Selected Interviews* (2001), *Paul Virilio: From Modernism to Hypermodernism and Beyond* (2000), and is currently completing *Virilio and the Media* and *Virilio Now: Current Perspectives in Virilio Studies*.

Bryan Finoki is the author of the blog *Subtopia: A Field Guide to Military Urbanism*. He lectures regularly and writes for newspapers and journals. He currently teaches at Woodbury University's School of Architecture in San Diego, California.

Frank Furedi is professor of sociology at the University of Kent in Canterbury. His research has focused on the culture of fear in relation to issues such as health, children, education, food, terrorism and new technologies. His most recent book is *Wasted: Why Education Is Not Educating* (2009).

Adi Kaplan and Shahar Carmel are artists based in Tel Aviv.

Gert Jan Kocken is an artist based in Amsterdam.

Wietske Maas lives in Amsterdam and works for the European Cultural Foundation. As an artist she is working (together with Matteo Pasquinelli) on the project *Urbanibalism*, which explores the gastronomic geography between the ecological fabrics of the city (www.urbanibalism.org).

Tom McCarthy is an artist and writer based in Londen. Tom McCarthy's novel *Remainder*, which deals with trauma and repetition, won the Believer Book Award 2007 and is currently being adapted for cinema. His new novel, C, which is about the relationship between technology and mourning, will be published in 2010.

Matteo Pasquinelli is a writer, curator and researcher at Queen Mary University in London. He wrote *Animal Spirits: A Bestiary of the Commons* (2008) and was an editor of *Media Activism* (2002) and *C'Lick Me: A Netporn Studies Reader* (2007). He writes frequently on French philosophy, media culture and Italian *postoperaismo*. He lives in Amsterdam.

Ilse van Rijn is an art historian. She works as a freelance writer together with artists and curators.

Brigitte van der Sande is an art historian and works as a freelance curator, editor and advisor.

Willem Schinkel lectures in theoretical sociology at the Erasmus University in Rotterdam. He is the author of *Denken in een tijd van sociale hypochondrie. Aanzet tot een theorie voor-*

bij de maatschappij (*Thinking in an Era of Social Hypochondria. Toward a Theory Beyond Society*, 2007).

<u>Bianca Stigter</u> is an art critic who writes for *NRC Handelsblad*, among other things. *Bezette stad. Plattegrond van Amsterdam 1940–1945* (*Occupied City. Map of Amsterdam 1940–1945*) was published in 2005.

<u>Kathleen Vandeputte</u> graduated in philosophy at the University of Ghent in 2004 and is working on a dissertation entitled 'From Communicide to Sensus Communis: The Depoliticisation of Community in Post-Totalitarian Political-Philosophical Thought'.

<u>Dirk van Weelden</u> is a writer and philosopher. His works include *Mobilhome* (1991), *Orville* (1997), *Looptijd* (2003), *Het middel* (2007) and *De wereld van 609* (2009).

<u>Willem van Weelden</u> is an artist, researcher and writer.

<u>Eyal Weizman</u> is an architect based in London. He is the director of the Centre for Research Architecture at Goldsmiths College (roundtable. kein.org). Since 2007 he has been a member of the architectural collective 'decolonizing architecture' in Beit Sahour/Palestine (www.decolonizing.ps). His books include *The Lesser Evil* (2009), *Hollow Land* (2007), *A Civilian Occupation* (2003) and the series *Territories 1, 2 and 3*.

CREDITS

Open Cahier on Art and
the Public Domain
Volume 8 (2009) no. 18

Editors Jorinde Seijdel (editor
in chief), Liesbeth Melis (final
editing)

Guest editor Brigitte van der Sande,
curator of 2030: War Zone Amsterdam

English copy editor D'Laine Camp

Dutch-English translations
Jane Bemont (editorial, text by
Willem Schinkel, introduction by
Brigitte van der Sande, introduc-
tion by Bianca Stigter; letter from
Amsterdam by Dirk van Weelden);
Michael Gibbs (book reviews by Ilse
van Rijn, Kathleen Vandeputte,
Willem van Weelden)
Hebrew-English Ruvik Daniely (text
artists' contribution Kaplan and
Carmel)

Graphic design Thomas Buxó and
Klaartje van Eijk

Printing and lithography Die Keure,
Brugge

Project coordinator Marieke van
Giersbergen, NAi Publishers

Publisher Eelco van Welie, NAi
Publishers

Open is published twice a year
Open 19 will be published in May 2010

Editorial address
SKOR
Ruysdaelkade 2
1072 AG Amsterdam
the Netherlands
Tel +31 (0)20 6722525
Fax +31 (0)20 3792809
open@skor.nl / www.opencahier.nl

SUBSCRIPTIONS

Abonnementenland
Postbus 20
1910 AA Uitgeest
the Netherlands
0900-2265263 – € 0,10 per minute)
Fax +31 (0)251 310405
www.aboland.nl.

PRICE PER ISSUE

€ 28.50

SUBSCRIPTION PRICES

(postage included)
the Netherlands: € 39.50
Within Europe: € 49.00
Outside Europe: € 55.00
Students: € 29.50

SUBSCRIPTION CANCELLATION

Cancellations (in writing only) must
be received by Abonnementenland
eight weeks prior to the end of the
subscription period. Subscriptions
not cancelled in time are automatically renewed for one year.

open

*For a comprehensive overview of contents according to author,
article and theme, see www.opencahier.nl*

(IN)SECURITY

(NO)MEMORY

(IN)VISIBILITY

SOUND

(IN)TOLERANCE

HYBRID SPACE

FREEDOM OF
CULTURE

THE RISE OF THE
INFORMAL MEDIA

ART AS A
PUBLIC ISSUE

SOCIAL
ENGINEERING

THE ART BIENNIAL AS
A GLOBAL PHENOMENON

A PRECARIOUS
EXISTENCE

NAi Publishers is an internationally orientated
publisher specialized in developing, producing and
distributing books on architecture, visual arts and
related disciplines.
www.naipublishers.nl info@naipublishers.nl

It was not possible to find all the copyright holders
of the illustrations used. Interested parties are
requested to contact NAi Publishers, Mauritsweg 23,
3012 JR Rotterdam, The Netherlands.

Available in North, South and Central America through
D.A.P./Distributed Art Publishers Inc, 155 Sixth
Avenue 2nd Floor, New York, NY 10013-1507, Tel 212
6271999, Fax 212 6279484.

Available in the United Kingdom and Ireland through
Art Data, 12 Bell Industrial Estate, 50 Cunnington
Street, London W4 5HB, Tel 208 7471061, Fax 208
7422319.

Printed and bound in Belgium

ISSN 1570-4181
ISBN 978-90-5662-710-2